CRYPTO RICH:

Guide To Transforming Investments Into Crypto Millions

BY

CHARLIE ANDREWS

CONTENT

Foreword

Welcome to the thrilling world of cryptocurrency investing—a realm where traditional finance meets cutting-edge technology, and fortunes are forged in the digital fires of innovation. In "CRYPTO RICH: Transforming Investments into Crypto Millions," you are about to embark on a journey that transcends conventional investment wisdom and delves into the dynamic landscape of crypto wealth creation.

As the global financial paradigm undergoes a revolutionary shift, the allure of cryptocurrencies has captured the imagination of investors worldwide. This book is your compass through the intricate terrain of digital assets, providing insights, strategies, and real-world stories illuminating the path to crypto riches.

In these pages, you will discover the foundational principles of cryptocurrency, demystify the blockchain technology that underpins it all, and explore a myriad of investment strategies tailored for both the cautious and the daring. From long-term hodlers to savvy day traders, "CRYPTO RICH" caters to the diverse spectrum of crypto enthusiasts, offering practical guidance for every stage of your investment journey.

The crypto market is not without its challenges, and the book equips you with the knowledge to navigate regulatory complexities, secure your assets, and mitigate risks effectively. Through the lens of success stories and cautionary tales, you'll gain valuable insights into the mindset and decisions that propel investors into the coveted realm of crypto millions.

Whether you're a seasoned investor or a curious newcomer, the future of finance is shaped by blockchain technology and digital currencies, and "CRYPTO RICH" is your indispensable companion on this transformative expedition. Embrace the opportunities, learn from the experiences shared within these pages, and empower yourself to make informed decisions in the ever-evolving world of crypto investments.

As you embark on this exciting adventure, may your understanding deepen, your confidence soars, and your investments flourish, turning your journey through the pages of "CRYPTO RICH" into a roadmap for your financial success in the crypto realm.
Happy investing!

Charlie Andrews

1. Introduction

In the early days of the 21st century, a mysterious figure known only by the pseudonym Satoshi Nakamoto ignited a spark that would set the financial world ablaze. From the ashes of economic crises and growing dissatisfaction with traditional banking systems, Nakamoto envisioned a decentralized currency that transcended borders and governments—a currency born of the digital age, powered by blockchain technology. Little did the world know that this vision would evolve into a global phenomenon, shaping the destiny of countless individuals and sparking a financial revolution that reverberates to this day.

As we traverse the pages of "CRYPTO RICH: Transforming Investments into Crypto Millions," we embark on a journey that mirrors the genesis of Bitcoin itself—a journey marked by innovation, uncertainty, and the unwavering belief in the transformative power of cryptocurrency. Our expedition begins not with the clang of traditional bells on Wall Street but with the hum of servers, the whir of algorithms, and the tapping of keys in the virtual realm.

Chapter by chapter, we peel back the layers of complexity surrounding cryptocurrency, demystifying the enigma that is Satoshi Nakamoto and the creation of Bitcoin. We delve into the inner workings of blockchain—the technology that birthed a new era in finance—and explore the evolution of a market that is as dynamic as it is disruptive.

The narrative unfolds with an exploration of the fundamental principles of cryptocurrency, laying the groundwork for readers to comprehend the intricacies of this digital frontier. We navigate the landscape of crypto investments, guided by the principles of long-term vision, diversification, and risk management. The strategies outlined within these pages cater to investors of all stripes, from those who choose to patiently HODL to the daring souls who thrive in the fast-paced world of day trading.

A dedicated chapter on day trading, a realm where fortunes are made and lost in minutes, awaits you. Here, we draw inspiration from the adrenaline-fueled stories of those who have successfully navigated the tumultuous seas of daily market fluctuations using skill, analysis, and intuition.

Just as any epic tale has its heroes and anti-heroes, "CRYPTO RICH" introduces you to the pioneers and trailblazers of the crypto world. From the early adopters who saw the potential when Bitcoin was mere cents to the innovators who birthed groundbreaking projects, their stories serve as beacons of inspiration and cautionary signals, guiding you through the unpredictable currents of the market.

This book is not just a guide; it's a companion on your journey, offering insights into the regulatory challenges, security measures, and future trends that will shape the crypto landscape. As we explore these facets, we pay homage to Satoshi Nakamoto—the elusive creator who set this odyssey in motion. His identity may remain mysterious, but his impact on the financial world is undeniable.

So, fasten your seatbelts and prepare to traverse the uncharted territories of cryptocurrency investments. Through the stories, strategies, and lessons encapsulated within "CRYPTO RICH," you are not merely learning about a market; you are becoming a participant in a global phenomenon that is rewriting the rules of finance—one block at a time. Welcome to the crypto odyssey; may it lead you to the riches you seek.

Why Crypto Investments?

In the annals of financial history, there are moments when a seismic shift occurs, altering how individuals perceive and interact with money. The advent of cryptocurrency represents one such epochal transformation, a departure from the established norms of finance and a plunge into the uncharted waters of decentralized digital assets.

To understand why crypto investments have captured the imagination of a generation, we must first embark on a journey through time. In the aftermath of the 2008 financial crisis, a mysterious figure known as Satoshi Nakamoto introduced Bitcoin to the world. Nakamoto's vision, outlined in a whitepaper titled "Bitcoin: A Peer-to-Peer Electronic Cash System," challenged the very foundations of traditional banking. Bitcoin was conceived as a decentralized, peer-to-peer currency that operated on blockchain technology—a secure, transparent, and immutable ledger.

Cryptocurrency emerged as a beacon of hope for the unbanked and underbanked populations around the globe. With traditional financial systems riddled with barriers, crypto offered an alternative to transcending geographical boundaries. Anyone with an internet connection could access, send, and receive digital assets, democratizing financial services.

Traditional currencies are subject to the whims of central banks and governments. In contrast, cryptocurrencies operate on decentralized networks, reducing the influence of centralized authorities. This decentralization fosters financial autonomy and guards against manipulation and arbitrary decisions that can impact traditional currencies.

Bitcoin, often called digital gold, introduced the concept of a store of value in the digital realm. As a finite asset with a capped supply, Bitcoin gained traction as a hedge against inflation, echoing the properties traditionally attributed to precious metals like gold.

Beyond Bitcoin, the crypto space witnessed the tokenization of assets—real estate, art, stocks, and more. Blockchain technology facilitated the fractional ownership of traditionally illiquid assets, unlocking new avenues for investment and democratizing access to previously exclusive markets.

Blockchain is at the heart of cryptocurrencies—a distributed ledger that ensures transparency, security, and immutability. Blockchain technology extends far beyond currency, finding applications in supply chain management, healthcare, and voting systems. The promise of a trustless and decentralized infrastructure fueled the enthusiasm for blockchain and its myriad applications.

The meteoric rise of specific cryptocurrencies, exemplified by Bitcoin's surge in value, has captured the attention of investors seeking unparalleled returns. The potential for exponential gains, albeit accompanied by heightened volatility, has drawn both seasoned investors and newcomers to the crypto market.

As traditional portfolios face challenges, investors are turning to cryptocurrencies to diversify. The lack of direct correlation with traditional asset classes positions cryptocurrencies as a unique addition to investment portfolios, potentially mitigating risk in market turbulence.

As we navigate the compelling landscape of cryptocurrency investments, it is crucial to approach this paradigm shift with a blend of curiosity, caution, and a commitment to understanding the underlying technologies. In the subsequent chapters of "CRYPTO RICH," we will delve deeper into the strategies, risks, and nuances that characterize the world of crypto investments, guiding you on a path that transcends traditional financial boundaries and ventures into digital wealth creation.

So, fasten your seatbelts as we embark on this odyssey, exploring the "why" behind crypto investments and unraveling the potential within this dynamic and transformative space. The journey has just begun, and the possibilities are as vast as the digital universe.

The Potential of Cryptocurrency

In the ever-evolving landscape of finance, the emergence of cryptocurrency stands as a transformative force, challenging traditional notions and unlocking a myriad of possibilities. In this chapter, we will delve into the potential of cryptocurrency, exploring its multifaceted impact on economies, industries, and the fabric of financial transactions.

Cryptocurrencies, operating on decentralized networks, have the potential to revolutionize cross-border transactions. With traditional financial systems often bogged down by intermediary banks, bureaucratic processes, and time delays, cryptocurrencies offer a streamlined alternative that enables near-instantaneous transfers, reducing costs and enhancing efficiency.

A staggering number of individuals worldwide lack access to traditional banking services. Cryptocurrencies, with their decentralized nature and accessibility through digital devices, provide an avenue for financial inclusion. The unbanked and underbanked populations can now participate in the global economy, opening doors to economic opportunities previously beyond reach.

At the core of cryptocurrency lies decentralization—a departure from centralized authorities and intermediaries. Blockchain technology, the backbone of cryptocurrencies, enables trustless systems where transactions are verified by a network of participants rather than relying on a single authority. This reduces the risk of fraud and fosters a more transparent and accountable financial ecosystem.

Cryptocurrency empowers individuals to have greater control over their financial assets. Posing private keys grants autonomy, eliminating the need for reliance on third-party institutions. This shift in control aligns with the ethos of economic sovereignty, allowing individuals to be the sole custodians of their wealth.

Smart contracts, self-executing contracts with the terms of the agreement directly written into code, have emerged as a groundbreaking application of blockchain technology. These programmable contracts automate and enforce the execution of predefined conditions, eliminating the need for intermediaries and reducing the potential for disputes.

The programmability of money through intelligent contracts has unleashed a wave of innovation. Decentralized Finance (DeFi) platforms, decentralized autonomous organizations (DAOs), and non-fungible tokens (NFTs) are just a few examples of how cryptocurrency is fostering creativity, collaboration, and entirely new economic ecosystems.

While transactions on traditional financial platforms are often subject to surveillance, specific cryptocurrencies prioritize user privacy. Privacy coins and features like confidential transactions and ring signatures enable users to conduct transactions with a greater degree of anonymity.

Blockchain's inherent security features make cryptocurrency transactions resistant to fraud and hacking. Cryptographic principles, consensus mechanisms, and decentralized networks contribute to a robust security infrastructure, instilling confidence in users to transact in the digital realm.

Cryptocurrencies enable the tokenization of assets, breaking down traditional barriers to entry in investment markets. Real estate, art, stocks, and commodities can be represented as tokens on the blockchain, providing fractional ownership opportunities to a broader range of investors.

Tokenization enhances liquidity, allowing assets to be traded more easily. Moreover, the fractional ownership model makes high-value assets accessible to a broader audience, democratizing investment opportunities and reshaping the landscape of wealth creation.

The developing nature of the crypto market is accompanied by volatility, presenting both opportunities and risks. Understanding market dynamics, conducting thorough research, and implementing risk management strategies are imperative for navigating this dynamic landscape.

As cryptocurrencies gain mainstream attention, regulatory frameworks are evolving. Navigating this shifting landscape requires vigilance, compliance, and an understanding of the legal implications of crypto investments.

As we peer into the potential of cryptocurrency, it becomes evident that we stand at the threshold of a financial revolution. Speed, efficiency, decentralization, programmability, and inclusivity position cryptocurrencies not merely as a speculative asset class but as catalysts for reshaping the foundations of how we exchange value.

In the ensuing chapters of "CRYPTO RICH," we will explore the practical aspects of harnessing this potential, crafting strategies to navigate the challenges, and embracing the transformative power of cryptocurrency investments. The journey has only begun, and this decentralized digital frontier has boundless potential for innovation and wealth creation.

Overview of the Book

Welcome to "CRYPTO RICH: Transforming Investments into Crypto Millions." In this comprehensive guide, we journeyed through the dynamic and transformative world of cryptocurrency investments. Whether you are a seasoned investor looking to diversify your portfolio or a curious newcomer seeking to understand the nuances of the crypto market, this book serves as your roadmap to navigating the complexities, seizing opportunities, and transforming your investments into crypto millions.

We begin our journey by exploring the fundamental question: Why Crypto Investments? Unravel the origins of cryptocurrency, understand its potential, and discover why it has captured the imagination of investors globally. From the mysterious beginnings of Bitcoin to the potential for financial inclusion, we lay the groundwork for a deeper understanding of the crypto landscape.

Delve into the multifaceted potential of cryptocurrency, exploring its impact on financial transactions, governance, and the fabric of our economic systems. From swift cross-border transactions to the programmability of money through smart contracts, we unveil the revolutionary aspects of crypto that are reshaping the future of finance.

For those taking their first steps into the crypto realm, Chapter 3 serves as a practical guide. Learn how to set up a cryptocurrency wallet, choose the proper exchange, and implement essential security measures. This chapter lays the foundation for a secure and informed entry into crypto investments.

With the basics in place, we dive into the strategies that can shape your crypto investment journey. Whether you lean towards long-term holdings, diversification, or day trading, Chapter 4 provides insights into crafting effective strategies that align with your risk tolerance and financial goals.

Navigate the sea of cryptocurrencies with confidence. Learn the art of researching and analyzing projects, conducting fundamental and technical analyses, and identifying promising investment opportunities. Chapter 5 equips you with the tools to make informed decisions in a market filled with diverse and dynamic projects.

Explore the ICOs and token sales world—where groundbreaking projects seek support. From understanding the concept of ICOs to evaluating project viability and managing the associated risks, Chapter 6 guides you through the intricacies of participating in these fundraising events.

For those with an appetite for the fast-paced trading world, Chapter 7 is dedicated to day trading strategies. From setting up a trading plan to mastering technical analysis, this chapter provides a comprehensive guide for those looking to capitalize on short-term market movements.

Understanding the legal considerations becomes crucial as the crypto space intersects with regulatory landscapes globally. Chapter 8 explores the regulatory challenges, tax implications, and legal frameworks that crypto investors need to navigate for a secure and compliant investment journey.

Safeguard your crypto assets with the insights shared in Chapter 9. From protecting your digital assets to identifying and avoiding common scams, this chapter offers practical advice on securing your investments and mitigating risks in the crypto space.

Gain inspiration and insights from the journeys of crypto millionaires. Chapter 10 presents real-world success stories, lessons learned from failures, and a glimpse into the mindset of those who have navigated the crypto landscape to achieve financial success.

Peer into the crystal ball and explore the emerging trends and predictions for the future of cryptocurrency. Chapter 11 examines the evolving landscape, technological advancements, and the adaptive strategies needed to thrive in the ever-changing crypto market.

As we approach the conclusion, Chapter 12 summarizes key concepts and encourages future crypto investors. Reflect on the knowledge gained and prepare to embark on your journey towards crypto riches.

Round off your learning experience with the appendix, featuring a glossary of cryptocurrency terms, additional resources for further exploration, and recommended reading to deepen your understanding of the crypto world.

This book is more than a guide; it is your companion in pursuing crypto riches. Each chapter is crafted to empower you with knowledge, strategies, and insights that will guide you through crypto investments' intricate and exciting landscape. So, let the journey begin—your venture into the world of crypto millions awaits.

2. Understanding Cryptocurrency

The hum of technology reverberated through the air, and a young professional named Alex found themselves at a crossroads. The world of finance, once a familiar landscape dominated by traditional banks and tangible currencies, was undergoing a profound metamorphosis.

Alex, armed with curiosity and a thirst for financial knowledge, embarked on a quest to unravel the mysteries of cryptocurrency. The journey began not in the hallowed halls of a financial institution but in the boundless realm of the internet, where the concept of digital currency was gaining momentum.

During this digital dawn, Alex discovered the story of Satoshi Nakamoto—an enigmatic figure whose identity remained shrouded in secrecy. Satoshi, like a modern-day alchemist, had introduced Bitcoin to the world. A decentralized currency, not tethered to any government or financial institution, Bitcoin sparked a revolution that challenged the very foundations of traditional finance.

As Alex delved deeper into cryptocurrency's genesis, the significance of understanding this new paradigm became increasingly apparent. The need for a global, decentralized currency was undeniable in a world where information traveled at the speed of light and traditional borders seemed to blur.

To comprehend the significance of cryptocurrency, Alex had to grasp the underlying technology—the blockchain. This distributed ledger, immutable and transparent, became the backbone of digital currencies. It promised secure and efficient financial transactions and transparency that traditional banking systems could only dream of.

Blockchain, Alex realized, was not just about currency; it was about trust. In an era plagued by data breaches and skepticism towards centralized authorities, blockchain offered a solution that resonated with the modern ethos of transparency and decentralization.

As Alex immersed themselves in cryptocurrency's intricacies, they unearthed this digital revolution's global nature. Cryptocurrencies, accessible to anyone with an internet connection, transcended borders and provided financial autonomy to individuals in regions where traditional banking systems had faltered.

Alex pondered the implications of financial inclusion—a world where anyone, regardless of geographic location or economic status, could participate in the global economy. Cryptocurrency was not just a medium of exchange but a catalyst for breaking down barriers and fostering a more inclusive financial landscape.

The more Alex learned, the more they realized that cryptocurrency wasn't just an alternative currency but a new asset class that could reshape investment portfolios. The finite nature of cryptocurrencies like Bitcoin, often called digital gold, sparked a paradigm shift in how individuals viewed stores of value.

In a world grappling with economic uncertainties and the erosion of traditional financial models, the emergence of a decentralized and scarce asset offered a beacon of stability and a hedge against inflation.

As Alex journeyed through the intricacies of cryptocurrency, the importance of understanding this new financial frontier became clear. In an age where digital transformation was not a luxury but a necessity, being equipped with the knowledge of blockchain, cryptocurrency, and their implications was akin to possessing a key to the future.

The digital age demanded a financial evolution that embraced decentralization, transparency, and inclusivity. For Alex and countless others navigating the complexities of the modern age, understanding cryptocurrency wasn't just a choice; it was a vital step towards financial empowerment and participation in a global economic landscape undergoing a tectonic shift.

Unraveling the strategies, risks, and triumphs that awaited in cryptocurrency. Little did they know that their quest for understanding would lead to financial knowledge and a transformation echoing a new era's pulse.

What is Cryptocurrency?

In the corners of the internet, where code hummed and digital transactions whispered through the virtual corridors, cryptocurrency emerged like a digital phoenix, rising from the ashes of traditional finance. As we embark on the second chapter of our journey through "CRYPTO RICH: Transforming Investments into Crypto Millions," we unravel the enigma encapsulated in the question, "What is Cryptocurrency?"

At its core, cryptocurrency is a manifestation of a decentralized, peer-to-peer system that transcends the traditional realms of banking and government-controlled currencies. In the aftermath of the 2008 financial crisis, the pseudonymous Satoshi Nakamoto introduced the world to the concept of a currency existing beyond the control of central authorities—a currency named Bitcoin.

Cryptocurrency is an amalgamation of two crucial elements: "crypto" and "currency." The term "crypto" refers to the cryptographic principles underpinning the security of these digital assets. Complex algorithms and mathematical functions ensure the integrity and confidentiality of transactions in a realm where trust is not placed in a central authority but instead in the verifiable and transparent nature of the blockchain.

The term "currency" signifies the function of these digital assets as mediums of exchange, units of account, and stores of value. Cryptocurrencies aim to emulate the functions of traditional currencies but with a distinctly digital and decentralized twist.

The blockchain is central to the concept of cryptocurrency—a revolutionary technology that acts as an incorruptible ledger, recording transactions across a network of computers. Each block in the chain contains a cryptographic hash of the previous block, creating a linked sequence resistant to tampering and revision.

The blockchain ensures transparency and security in a trustless environment. Every transaction is visible to participants in the network, creating a level of accountability that challenges the opacity of traditional financial systems.

Unlike traditional financial transactions that rely on banks as intermediaries, cryptocurrency transactions occur directly between users. When Alice wants to send cryptocurrency to Bob, the transaction is broadcast to the network. Miners, the decentralized entities responsible for validating transactions, ensure its legitimacy. Once verified, the transaction is added to a block, and the blockchain is updated.

The use of public and private keys adds a layer of security. Public keys, akin to an address, are visible to all, while private keys, known only to the owner, are used to sign transactions, providing a secure means of ownership verification.

While Bitcoin remains the pioneering cryptocurrency, the digital landscape has witnessed the emergence of thousands of alternative cryptocurrencies, often referred to as altcoins. Each has its unique features, purposes, and underlying technologies. Ethereum, for instance, introduced smart contracts, enabling programmable and self-executing agreements on its blockchain.

Bitcoin, in particular, operates on a deflationary model with a capped supply of 21 million coins. This scarcity starkly contrasts traditional fiat currencies, which central banks can print in unlimited quantities. "mining" involves solving complex mathematical problems to validate transactions and add them to the blockchain. Miners are rewarded with newly minted cryptocurrency, a mechanism that secures the network and introduces new units into circulation.

In the decentralized world of cryptocurrency, achieving consensus—unanimous agreement on the state of the blockchain—is paramount. Different consensus mechanisms, such as Proof of Work (PoW) and Proof of Stake (PoS), have emerged as solutions to this challenge. These mechanisms dictate how transactions are verified, blocks are added to the chain, and, in the case of PoW, how mining is conducted.

To navigate the world of cryptocurrencies, users need a digital wallet—a secure repository for storing private keys. Wallets come in various forms, including software, hardware, and paper wallets. Each offers a trade-off between convenience and security, allowing users to choose the solution that best aligns with their needs and preferences.

Cryptocurrencies, with their decentralized and speculative nature, are known for their price volatility. While this volatility presents investment opportunities, it also introduces risks. Yet, this dynamic environment has also fostered a culture of innovation. From decentralized finance (DeFi) to non-fungible tokens (NFTs), the crypto space is a hotbed of creativity and experimentation.

In concluding our exploration of "What is Cryptocurrency?" it becomes evident that these digital assets represent more than a technological novelty. Cryptocurrency embodies a paradigm shift in perceiving, transacting, and storing value. It challenges the very foundations of traditional finance, offering a glimpse into a future where financial systems are transparent, inclusive, and decentralized.

In the subsequent chapters of "CRYPTO RICH," we delve deeper into the practical aspects of cryptocurrency investments. From understanding investment strategies to navigating regulatory challenges, our journey continues, guided by the foundational knowledge of what cryptocurrency truly is—a digital revolution that has already begun reshaping the landscape of wealth and finance.

How Blockchain Technology Works

As we embark on Chapter 3 of "CRYPTO RICH: Transforming Investments into Crypto Millions," let us unravel how this transformative technology underpins the essence of cryptocurrencies.

At its core, blockchain is a decentralized and distributed ledger—a digital record of transactions duplicated and spread across the entire network of computer systems participating in a cryptocurrency ecosystem. Each unit of information, or "block," contains a list of transactions, a timestamp, and a reference to the previous block, creating an immutable and chronological chain.

The primary purpose of a block is to store transactional information. When a user initiates a cryptocurrency transaction, it is grouped with others into a block.

Each block contains a timestamp, recording the exact moment the transactions were added to the ledger. This chronological order is crucial for maintaining the integrity and consistency of the blockchain.

One of the defining features of blockchain is its immutability. Achieved through cryptographic hash functions, each block's hash is generated based on its content, including the previous block's hash. If someone attempts to alter a block, it would require changing the information in that block and all subsequent blocks—a near-impossible feat.

The "nonce" is a random number added to the block during mining. Miners adjust this number until they find a hash that meets specific criteria, a process known as proof of work. The nonce adds an element of randomness, making it computationally infeasible to predict or manipulate the outcome.

The strength of blockchain lies in its linking mechanism. Each block contains the previous block's hash, forming a continuous chain of blocks. This chain structure ensures that once a block is added to the ledger, it becomes an integral part of the historical record.

Unlike traditional centralized databases controlled by a single entity, blockchain operates on a decentralized network. Copies of the entire blockchain exist on multiple nodes (computers) spread across the network. Each node has its copy of the ledger, and consensus mechanisms ensure that all copies remain in sync.

Various consensus mechanisms are employed to maintain the integrity of the blockchain and establish agreement among nodes. Two common mechanisms are:

In PoW, miners compete to solve complex mathematical problems. The first solution to the problem is the right to add a new block to the blockchain. This process requires significant computational power, ensuring that adding a block is resource-intensive and time-consuming.

PoS, on the other hand, selects the creator of a new block based on their ownership or stake in the cryptocurrency. The more coins a participant holds, the more likely they will be chosen to create a new block. PoS is considered more energy-efficient compared to PoW.

The immutability of blockchain is a direct result of cryptographic hashing and consensus mechanisms. Once a block is added to the chain, altering its information would require changing subsequent blocks. This task becomes computationally infeasible due to the decentralized and distributed nature of the network.

Blockchain technology extends beyond currency transactions. Smart contracts, self-executing contracts with the terms of the agreement directly written into code, enable complex transactions and agreements without intermediaries. Ethereum, with its Turing-complete scripting language, brought the concept of smart contracts into the mainstream.

In the blockchain realm, a "fork" occurs when a blockchain diverges into two separate paths. This can be planned, as in the case of a software upgrade, or unplanned due to a disagreement within the network. Forks highlights the democratic nature of blockchain, where consensus is essential for the continued integrity of the ledger.

While blockchain technology offers unprecedented security and transparency, it has challenges. Scalability, the ability to handle a growing number of transactions, remains a concern. Various projects are actively working on solutions, such as layer-two scaling solutions and alternative consensus mechanisms.

As we conclude our exploration of blockchain technology, it is crucial to recognize its potential beyond cryptocurrencies. Blockchain is a foundational technology with applications in supply chain management, healthcare, voting systems, and more. Its decentralized, transparent, and secure nature makes it a catalyst for innovation across industries.

In the chapters ahead, we will delve deeper into the practical applications of blockchain technology and how it forms the backbone of the cryptocurrency ecosystem. Understanding blockchain mechanics is not just a technical endeavor; it is a key that unlocks the doors to a decentralized future where trust, transparency, and security redefine how we interact with information and value.

Key Cryptocurrencies in the Market

The vast expanse of the cryptocurrency market, a constellation of digital assets, sparkles with potential, each contributing a unique hue to the cosmic landscape. As we traverse Chapter 5 of "CRYPTO RICH: Transforming Investments into Crypto Millions," let us explore the key cryptocurrencies that dominate this dynamic realm.

Bitcoin, the progenitor of this digital revolution, stands at the forefront of the cryptocurrency universe. Conceived by the mysterious Satoshi Nakamoto, Bitcoin introduced the concept of decentralized, peer-to-peer currency. As digital gold, Bitcoin is valued not only for its utility as a medium of exchange but also for its scarcity—capped at 21 million coins, echoing the attributes of precious metals.

Store of Value: Bitcoin is often called digital gold, immune to the inflationary pressures that affect traditional fiat currencies.

Decentralization: The decentralized nature of Bitcoin ensures resilience against manipulation by central authorities.

Halving: Approximately every four years, the reward for mining new Bitcoin blocks is halved, reducing the rate at which new coins are introduced.

In the cosmic dance of cryptocurrencies, Ethereum emerges as a star with transformative capabilities. Beyond its role as a digital currency, Ethereum introduced intelligent contracts—self-executing agreements coded directly onto the blockchain. This innovation unlocked a realm of possibilities, giving rise to decentralized applications (DApps) and fueling the era of decentralized finance (DeFi).

Smart Contracts: Ethereum's scripting language enables the creation of programmable contracts, automating complex agreements without intermediaries.

Decentralized Applications (DApps): Ethereum provides the foundation for decentralized applications across various industries.

EIP-1559: Ethereum Improvement Proposal 1559 aims to address scalability and transaction fee concerns through a new fee mechanism.

As a celestial companion in crypto, Binance Coin orbits the Binance ecosystem, one of the largest cryptocurrency exchanges globally. Originally an Ethereum-based token, BNB transitioned to Binance Chain, evolving into a utility token with diverse use cases within the Binance ecosystem.

Utility Token: BNB serves various purposes within the Binance ecosystem, including trading fee discounts, participation in token sales, and access to decentralized finance services.

Binance Smart Chain (BSC): BNB powers transactions and operations on Binance Smart Chain, facilitating faster and more affordable transactions than Ethereum.

Cardano shines as a project grounded in scientific philosophy in the cosmic expanse of blockchain innovation. Founded by academics and engineers, Cardano employs a meticulous, research-driven approach to build a scalable and sustainable blockchain platform.

Proof-of-Stake (PoS): Cardano utilizes a PoS consensus mechanism, aiming for sustainability and energy efficiency.

Layers of the Platform: Cardano is designed in layers, separating the ledger into the Cardano Settlement Layer (CSL) for transactions and the Cardano Computation Layer (CCL) for smart contracts.

Ripple shines as a solution for cross-border payments and remittances in the stellar tapestry of cryptocurrencies. RippleNet, the network underpinning XRP, facilitates fast and cost-effective international transactions.

Digital Payment Protocol: Ripple serves as a digital currency (XRP) and a payment protocol, providing a seamless solution for global money transfers.

Partnerships: Ripple has established partnerships with financial institutions and banks worldwide to enhance cross-border payment solutions.

In the evolving galaxy of blockchain ecosystems, Solana emerges as a high-performance blockchain designed to handle many transactions quickly and cost-effectively. With its focus on scalability, Solana aims to support decentralized applications with minimal transaction fees.

High Throughput: Solana boasts high throughput, processing thousands of transactions per second.

Proof-of-History (PoH): Solana's unique PoH mechanism enhances the efficiency of transaction validation, contributing to its scalability.

As we traverse the interconnected galaxies of blockchain networks, Polkadot emerges as a pioneer in interoperability. Founded by Dr. Gavin Wood, one of Ethereum's co-founders, Polkadot facilitates communication and collaboration between disparate blockchains.

Interoperability: Polkadot's relay chain connects different blockchains, enabling them to share information and assets seamlessly.

Parachains: Polkadot introduces the concept of parachains—individual blockchains that connect to the Polkadot network, each with its specific use case.

In the ever-expanding universe of decentralized applications, Chainlink orbits as a decentralized oracle network. Its role is to connect smart contracts with real-world data, enabling them to interact with external information securely and trustlessly.

Decentralized Oracles: Chainlink provides a decentralized oracle network, ensuring the reliability and accuracy of external data fed into smart contracts.

Broad Integration: Chainlink is widely integrated into various blockchain projects, enhancing the functionality of decentralized applications.

In the cosmic metaphor of digital assets, Litecoin often plays the role of silver to Bitcoin's gold. Created by Charlie Lee, a former Google engineer, Litecoin shares many similarities with Bitcoin but distinguishes itself with faster block generation times and a different hashing algorithm.

Scrypt Algorithm: Litecoin uses the Scrypt algorithm, which is designed to be memory-intensive and resistant to ASIC mining.

Segregated Witness (SegWit): Litecoin was among the early adopters of SegWit, a protocol upgrade to improve transaction malleability and increase block capacity.

Stellar shines as a beacon of financial inclusion in the vast galaxy of blockchain projects. With a mission to connect people and institutions through efficient and low-cost cross-border payments,

Stellar's lumens (XLM) serve as both a digital currency and a bridge between fiat currencies.

Stellar Consensus Protocol (SCP): Stellar operates on SCP, a consensus mechanism designed for fast and secure transaction validation.

Anchor System: Stellar's anchor system facilitates the exchange of various assets, enabling seamless cross-border transactions.

5.11 Uniswap (UNI): The Decentralized Exchange Pioneer in the dynamic ecosystem of decentralized finance (DeFi), Uniswap emerges as a pioneering force. As a decentralized exchange (DEX) built on the Ethereum blockchain, Uniswap facilitates the seamless and permissionless swapping of various ERC-20 tokens.

Automated Market Maker (AMM): Uniswap employs an AMM model, allowing users to trade directly from their wallets without needing a centralized intermediary.

Liquidity Pools: Users can contribute liquidity to pools and earn fees, contributing to the decentralized liquidity ecosystem.

In the cosmic tapestry of cryptocurrencies, Dogecoin orbits as a playful and community-driven digital asset. Initially created as a lighthearted meme, Dogecoin has garnered a devoted following and gained recognition for its charitable endeavors.

Community Engagement: Dogecoin's vibrant community has often rallied behind charitable causes and social initiatives.

Inflationary Model: Unlike Bitcoin, Dogecoin has no maximum supply, with a capped yearly issuance to prevent excessive inflation.

5.14 ChainSol (CHS): The Hybrid Blockchain Emissary

In the celestial ensemble of cryptocurrencies, ChainSol emerges as a hybrid blockchain, seamlessly blending the strengths of public and private blockchain architectures. We were founded on the principles of security, scalability, and privacy. ChainSol endeavors to bridge the gap between decentralized transparency and enterprise-grade solutions.

5.14.1 Notable Characteristics:

- **Hybrid Architecture:** ChainSol integrates the transparency and decentralization of public blockchains with the privacy and control features of private blockchains.
- **Interoperability:** ChainSol is designed to interoperate with various existing blockchain networks, fostering collaboration across diverse ecosystems.
- **Enterprise-Focused:** With an emphasis on catering to enterprise needs, ChainSol offers solutions for secure data management, supply chain optimization, and confidential transactions.

It becomes evident that the crypto cosmos is a vibrant and diverse ecosystem. Each digital asset contributes a unique value proposition, whether as a store of value, a platform for decentralized applications, or a solution for specific industries. The following chapters will delve deeper into the strategies for navigating this cosmic landscape. From understanding investment opportunities to crafting adequate portfolio diversification, our journey continues through the ever-expanding universe of cryptocurrency investments. So, fasten your seatbelts as we navigate the constellations of the crypto cosmos, seeking to transform investments into crypto millions.

3. Getting Started with Crypto Investments

Alex found themselves standing at the crossroads of tradition and innovation. The allure of crypto investments beckoned—an uncharted territory promising risks and untold rewards. With curiosity and a yearning for financial empowerment, Alex embarked on a journey into cryptocurrencies.

It all began one evening as Alex engrossed in an online financial forum, stumbled upon a thread discussing the transformative power of cryptocurrency. The mysterious allure of decentralized assets and the potential for substantial returns ignited a spark within Alex's financial imagination.

Intrigued, Alex started delving into the origins of cryptocurrencies, from the enigmatic creation of Bitcoin by Satoshi Nakamoto to the evolution of an entire ecosystem beyond the pioneering digital gold. The more they read, the more the desire to venture into this decentralized frontier intensified.

Eager to embark on their crypto odyssey, Alex knew the first step was crucial. Armed with determination, they set out to understand the practical aspects of getting started with crypto investments.

The journey commenced with selecting a reliable cryptocurrency exchange. Alex meticulously researched various platforms, weighing security, ease of use, and available features. After careful consideration, they chose a reputable exchange that offered a seamless onboarding experience.

Understanding the importance of security, Alex explored the realm of cryptocurrency wallets. They learned about the differences between hot wallets (connected to the internet) and cold wallets (offline), opting for a combination that prioritized convenience without compromising security.

With a wallet in hand, Alex initiated their maiden cryptocurrency transaction. The process, initially daunting, became an empowering experience. Alex marveled at the speed and efficiency of transferring digital assets across borders, unencumbered by traditional banking constraints.

As Alex navigated the crypto seas, they understood the significance of having a financial compass. Goals became the guiding stars, shaping the trajectory of their investments. Whether building a diversified portfolio, saving for a milestone, or exploring new opportunities, Alex's goals provided direction in the volatile world of cryptocurrencies.

Alex delved into the diverse strategies available for crypto investments, from the long-term HODLing philosophy to the dynamic world of day trading. Recognizing the need for a balanced approach, Alex crafted a strategy aligned with their risk tolerance and financial aspirations.

The art of researching and analyzing projects became an essential skill in Alex's toolkit. They honed their ability to distinguish promising cryptocurrencies from speculative ventures, delving into whitepapers, exploring community sentiment, and mastering fundamental and technical analyses.

Understanding the volatility inherent in the crypto market, Alex embraced the importance of risk management. Setting stop-loss orders, diversifying investments, and staying informed about market trends became integral to their risk mitigation strategy.

As Alex sailed more deeply into the crypto seas, they discovered the vibrant and passionate crypto community. Forums, social media groups, and local meetups became portals to share knowledge, experiences, and valuable insights. The camaraderie of fellow crypto enthusiasts provided support during market fluctuations and celebrated victories in unison.

Understanding the regulatory landscape became a pivotal part of Alex's journey. From tax implications to compliance with local laws, they navigated the regulatory waters diligently, ensuring that their crypto investments remained secure and compliant.

In the realm of digital assets, security was paramount. Alex implemented robust security measures, including two-factor authentication, hardware wallets, and regular cybersecurity audits. Safeguarding their crypto holdings became a daily ritual, reinforcing the resilience of their financial fortress.

As the chapters of Alex's crypto odyssey unfolded, the first glimpses of success illuminated their path. Whether through strategic investments, successful trades, or simply witnessing the growth of their portfolio, Alex felt the transformative power of crypto investments firsthand.

As Alex's journey continued, they gazed toward the crypto horizon. With newfound knowledge, strategic understanding, and a growing sense of financial empowerment, Alex stood at the forefront of a digital revolution—an explorer in a realm where traditional finance intersected with the future.

In the following chapters, Alex's odyssey delved deeper into the nuances of crypto investments. From identifying promising projects to navigating market trends, their narrative unfolded as a testament to the transformative potential of embracing the crypto frontier. Little did Alex know that the pages of their journey would tell a personal story and contribute to the collective narrative of a decentralized future.

Setting Up a Cryptocurrency Wallet

Setting up a cryptocurrency wallet is akin to forging a fortress to safeguard your digital assets. As we venture into Chapter 4 of "CRYPTO RICH: Transforming Investments into Crypto Millions," let us explore the meticulous process of crafting your vault, your gateway to the decentralized universe of cryptocurrencies. Before embarking on the journey of setting up a cryptocurrency wallet, one must understand the diverse landscape of wallet options. Cryptocurrency wallets come in various forms, each catering to different needs and preferences. The main categories include:

Online Wallets: Online wallets emerge as virtual sanctuaries, balancing accessibility and user-friendly interfaces. As we delve into Chapter 5 of "CRYPTO RICH: Transforming Investments into Crypto Millions," let us explore the world of online wallets, understand their nuances, and examine notable examples.

Online wallets, also known as web wallets or hot wallets, reside in the digital realm, accessible through web browsers or dedicated applications. Their appeal lies in their convenience, enabling users to easily manage their digital assets while maintaining quick access to funds. While security remains paramount, online wallets are often favored for their user-friendly interfaces and real-time connectivity.

Let's explore some of the prominent online wallets in the crypto landscape, each with unique features and characteristics.

Website: [Coinbase](https://www.coinbase.com/)
Coinbase is a widely recognized and user-friendly platform that serves as an exchange and an online wallet. It supports various cryptocurrencies, providing a seamless onboarding experience for beginners.

Blockchain.info (Blockchain Wallet)**
Website: [Blockchain. info](https://www.blockchain.com/)
As one of the earliest online wallets in the crypto space,
Blockchain.info offers a non-custodial wallet solution. Users control
their private keys, emphasizing security and privacy.

Website: [Binance](https://www.binance.com/)
Binance, a leading cryptocurrency exchange, also provides an
online wallet service. Users can seamlessly transition between
trading and storing assets within the Binance ecosystem.

Website: [Exodus](https://www.exodus.com/)
Known for its sleek design and intuitive interface, Exodus is a
software wallet that supports a variety of cryptocurrencies. It offers
a built-in exchange feature for seamless asset swaps.

Website: [Guarda Wallet](https://guarda.com/)
Guarda Wallet is a multi-currency online wallet that allows users to
manage a diverse range of cryptocurrencies. It offers both web
and mobile versions for flexibility.

Website: [Electrum](https://electrum.org/)
Electrum is a lightweight and secure Bitcoin wallet that operates as
a software wallet and offers a web version. It is known for its
speed and efficiency.

Website: [MyEtherWallet](https://www.myetherwallet.com/)
MyEtherWallet is a popular online wallet specifically designed for
Ethereum and Ethereum-based tokens. It provides a simple
interface for managing ERC-20 assets.

While online wallets offer convenience, users must prioritize
security to safeguard their digital assets. Here are essential
security considerations:

Enable 2FA to add an extra layer of security, requiring a secondary verification step for accessing your online wallet.

Ensure that the website uses HTTPS, indicating a secure connection. Avoid accessing wallets through unsecured or suspicious links.

Always secure and back up your recovery phrase in a safe and offline location. This phrase is crucial for restoring access in case of account recovery.

Keep your online wallet software up to date to benefit from the latest security patches and enhancements.

Online wallets serve as digital portals to the vast crypto universe, offering a blend of accessibility and functionality. Users must navigate this space with a keen understanding of security best practices while choosing platforms that align with their preferences.

We will delve deeper into the strategies for managing and growing your
cryptocurrency portfolio, whether it resides in the virtual sanctuaries of online wallets or explores other facets of the decentralized landscape. As you embark on your journey, may your online wallet be a secure vessel guiding you through the currents of the crypto seas.

Mobile Wallets: Mobile wallets, the superheroes of convenience, empower users to carry the magic of cryptocurrency wherever they go. Join us in Chapter 6 of "CRYPTO RICH: Transforming Investments into Crypto Millions" as we explore the world of mobile wallets, understand their dynamics, and unravel their potential.

Mobile wallets, often called wallet apps, bring a new level of accessibility to cryptocurrencies. With most of the global population owning smartphones, these mobile marvels transform any handheld device into a portal to the decentralized realm. The ability to manage, send, and receive digital assets on the go has become a defining feature of the crypto landscape.

Let's venture into the vibrant landscape of mobile wallets, each catering to the diverse needs of users while offering a seamless and portable crypto experience.

Website: [**Trust Wallet**](https://trustwallet.com/)

Acquired by Binance, Trust Wallet is a secure and user-friendly mobile wallet supporting many cryptocurrencies. Its simplicity and integration with the Binance Smart Chain make it a favorite among users.

Website: [**Coinomi**](https://www.coinomi.com/)

Coinomi is a mobile wallet known for its robust security features and support for many cryptocurrencies. It offers a user-friendly interface and emphasizes privacy.

Website: [Atomic Wallet](https://atomicwallet.io/)

Atomic Wallet is a decentralized mobile wallet that enables users to manage their portfolios and exchange assets seamlessly. Its built-in atomic swap feature allows for direct peer-to-peer trading.

Website: [**Edge Wallet**](https://edge.app/)

Edge Wallet stands out for its focus on user control and privacy. Users maintain control over their private keys, and the wallet supports a variety of cryptocurrencies.

Website: [**BRD**](https://brd.com/)

BRD, once known as Bread Wallet, is a simple and intuitive mobile wallet that prioritizes ease of use. It allows users to buy, store, and manage multiple cryptocurrencies.

Website: [**Enjin Wallet**](https://enjin.io/)

Enjin Wallet is designed to support blockchain-based gaming assets and non-fungible tokens (NFTs). It offers a sleek interface and integration with the Enjin ecosystem.

Website: [**Exodus**](https://www.exodus.com/)

While Exodus is a multi-platform wallet, its mobile version is noteworthy. It provides a sleek design and a user-friendly interface for managing a diverse range of cryptocurrencies.

Mobile wallets offer a range of features that enhance the user experience and cater to the evolving needs of the crypto community.

Mobile wallets often include QR code scanning functionality to simplify the process of sending and receiving cryptocurrencies.

Some mobile wallets integrate exchange features, allowing users to swap one cryptocurrency for another without leaving the app.

Many mobile wallets provide tools for tracking portfolio performance, displaying real-time balances and historical transaction data.

Mobile wallets often incorporate push notifications for activities such as fund deposits or withdrawals to keep users informed about their transactions.

While the convenience of mobile wallets is undeniable, ensuring the security of your digital assets is paramount. Consider the following security measures:

Enable biometric authentication, such as fingerprint or face recognition, to add an extra layer of security to your mobile wallet.

Always secure and store your wallet's recovery phrase in a safe and offline location. This phrase is crucial for recovering your purse in case of device loss.

Download mobile wallet apps only from official app stores to minimize the risk of downloading malicious software.

As we conclude our exploration of mobile wallets, remember that these digital companions bring the magic of cryptocurrencies to your fingertips. Whether managing a diversified portfolio or exploring the world of decentralized applications, mobile wallets bridge the physical and digital realms.

We will continue our journey, delving into strategies for maximizing the potential of your cryptocurrency investments. So, keep your mobile marvel at hand as we navigate the ever-evolving cosmos of crypto opportunities.

Desktop Wallets: Software installed on personal computers grants users you control over their private keys.

USB Devices: USB devices stand as guardians of your cryptocurrency assets. As we embark on Chapter 7 of "CRYPTO RICH: Transforming Investments into Crypto Millions," let us delve into the realm of USB devices, exploring their role as secure vaults for safeguarding digital wealth.

USB devices, often called hardware wallets, bridge the gap between the tangible and intangible. These compact devices provide an added layer of security by keeping private keys offline, reducing the vulnerability to online threats. Their physical nature adds a dimension of control and ownership to digital assets.

Let's navigate through the landscape of hardware wallets, each designed to focus on security, user experience, and functionality.

[Ledger] (https://www.ledger.com/)

Ledger Nano S and Nano X are the most popular hardware wallets globally. They support many cryptocurrencies, feature secure chip technology, and include a specific element for added protection.

[Trezor] (https://trezor.io/)

Trezor Model T and Trezor One are hardware wallets developed by SatoshiLabs. The Model T features a touchscreen interface, while the Trezor One provides a classic design. Both prioritize security and ease of use.

[KeepKey](https://www.keepkey.com/)

- **Overview:** KeepKey, acquired by ShapeShift, is a sleek hardware wallet known for its large screen and user-friendly interface. It supports various cryptocurrencies and emphasizes simplicity.

[Coldcard] (https://coldcardwallet.com/)

Coldcard is a hardware wallet designed for Bitcoin users, focusing on security and privacy. It features a unique air-gapped signing mechanism and supports advanced features like multi-signature wallets.

[BitBox] (https://shiftcrypto.ch/bitbox02/)

- **Overview:** BitBox offers both BitBox02 Multi Edition and BitBox02 Bitcoin-only Edition. It is known for its compact design, security features, and integration with the BitBoxApp for easy management.

USB devices have features that distinguish them as secure storage solutions for cryptocurrency holdings.

USB devices operate in a state of cold storage, meaning private keys remain offline, reducing exposure to online threats.

Many hardware wallets incorporate a secure element, a dedicated chip designed to enhance security and resist tampering.

USB devices often feature user-friendly interfaces, making them accessible even to those less familiar with the technical intricacies of cryptocurrencies.

Hardware wallets provide backup and recovery options through seed phrases, enabling users to restore access in case of device loss or failure.

Ensuring the security of USB devices is paramount to safeguarding your digital assets. Implement the following best practices:

Purchase from Official Sources

Obtain hardware wallets directly from official sources to mitigate the risk of receiving compromised devices.

Always verify the receiving address on the hardware wallet's screen before confirming transactions to prevent address substitution attacks.

Keep the firmware of your hardware wallet up to date to benefit from the latest security enhancements.

Set a strong PIN for your hardware wallet to prevent unauthorized access. Avoid using easily guessable combinations.

As we conclude our exploration of USB devices, remember that these compact guardians bridge the gap between cryptocurrency storage's physical and digital dimensions. Whether you opt for Ledger, Trezor, KeepKey, Coldcard, or BitBox, your choice reflects a commitment to the tangible security of your digital wealth. You are navigating through the diverse strategies for maximizing the potential of your cryptocurrency investments. So, let your USB device be the key to unlocking the vast opportunities within the crypto cosmos, securely anchored in the physical realm.

Hardware Cards: Compact and portable, these cards store cryptographic keys securely.

Physical Documents: Printed or written records of public and private keys, providing a tangible and offline storage solution. Choosing a wallet is a personalized decision that depends on security preferences, ease of use, and the level of control one wishes to maintain over their digital assets. For newcomers, simplicity and user-friendly interfaces are paramount, while seasoned users prioritize enhanced security features.

Cold Storage: Hardware wallets and paper wallets, being offline, offer enhanced security by protecting private keys from online threats.

Two-Factor Authentication (2FA): Wallets with 2FA provide an additional layer of protection, requiring a secondary verification step for access.

Intuitive Design: For beginners, wallets with intuitive interfaces simplify the process of sending and receiving cryptocurrencies.

Accessibility: Mobile wallets ensure access to digital assets on the go, while desktop wallets offer a comprehensive interface.

Self-Custody: Wallets that grant users control over their private keys align with the decentralized ethos of cryptocurrencies.

Third-Party Custody: Some wallets, mainly online wallets, manage private keys on behalf of users, sacrificing some control for convenience.

With an understanding of the wallet landscape and considerations, let's embark on the step-by-step journey of setting up a cryptocurrency wallet.

Select a wallet that aligns with your preferences and needs. For beginners, mobile wallets or user-friendly desktop wallets may be suitable, while those prioritizing security might opt for hardware or paper wallets.

Visit the official website or app store associated with your chosen wallet. Ensure you are downloading from a legitimate source to avoid potential security risks.

Follow the on-screen instructions to create your wallet. This often involves setting up a username and password and securing your recovery phrase. The recovery phrase, or seed phrase, is a crucial aspect of wallet security and serves as a backup to restore access if needed.

Store it in a secure and offline location upon generating your recovery phrase. This phrase is the key to restoring your wallet in case of device loss or failure.

Once your wallet is set up and secured, you can fund it by transferring cryptocurrencies from an exchange or another wallet. Ensure you are using the correct wallet address to prevent any loss of funds.

Many wallets offer additional features such as portfolio tracking, transaction history, and decentralized applications (DApps) integration. Take the time to explore these features to maximize the utility of your wallet.

Setting up a wallet is not the final step but the beginning of a continuous commitment to security. Implementing best practices ensures the longevity and safety of your digital assets.

Periodically back up your wallet, especially after making significant changes or additions. Store backup copies in multiple secure locations.

Regularly update your wallet software to benefit from the latest security enhancements and improvements.

Be cautious of phishing attempts and only access your wallet through official channels. Avoid clicking on suspicious links or providing sensitive information to unknown sources.

Remember that your wallet is more than a digital container—it is your gateway to financial empowerment and a fortress protecting your digital wealth. Choose wisely, prioritize security, and navigate the crypto seas confidently, knowing that your digital assets are safeguarded within the walls of your crypto vault. In the following chapters, we will delve deeper into the strategies and considerations for managing and growing your cryptocurrency portfolio within the secure confines of your chosen wallet.

Choosing the Right Cryptocurrency Exchange

Exchanges serve as the bustling marketplaces where digital assets change hands. As we embark on Chapter 8 of "CRYPTO RICH: Transforming Investments into Crypto Millions," we delve into the critical decision of selecting the suitable cryptocurrency exchange. This choice is akin to choosing the trading floor where your financial journey takes flight.

Cryptocurrency exchanges function as gateways, allowing users to buy, sell, and trade digital assets. Choosing the suitable exchange is pivotal, impacting factors such as security, accessibility, available assets, and the overall trading experience.

Let's explore a selection of cryptocurrency exchanges, each renowned for specific features and catering to diverse user preferences.

[Binance] (https://www.binance.com/)

Binance is a global cryptocurrency exchange known for its extensive range of tradable assets, competitive trading fees, and innovative features like Binance Launchpad for token sales.

[Coinbase] (https://www.coinbase.com/)

Coinbase is a user-friendly exchange that serves as a popular on-ramp for beginners. It offers a simple interface, various supported cryptocurrencies, and additional services like Coinbase Pro for advanced traders.

[Kraken] (https://r.kraken.com/c/2042870/687155/10583)
Kraken is a well-established exchange with a strong reputation for security. It provides a wide range of cryptocurrencies for trading, margin trading options, and futures trading.

[Gemini] (https://gemini.com/)
Founded by the Winklevoss twins, Gemini is a regulated exchange known for its emphasis on security and compliance. It offers a user-friendly interface and a range of supported cryptocurrencies.

[Bitstamp] (https://www.bitstamp.net/)
Bitstamp is one of the longest-standing cryptocurrency exchanges, known for its reliability and transparency. It supports a selection of significant cryptocurrencies and provides a straightforward trading platform.

When selecting a cryptocurrency exchange, various factors come into play. Consider the following aspects to make an informed decision:

Prioritize exchanges with robust security features, including two-factor authentication (2FA), cold storage for funds, and a transparent security track record.

Ensure that the exchange supports the cryptocurrencies you intend to trade. Some exchanges focus on a broad range, while others specialize in specific assets.

Evaluate the fee structure of the exchange, including trading fees, withdrawal fees, and deposit fees. Look for transparent fee policies to avoid unexpected charges.

Consider the user interface of the exchange, especially if you are a beginner. A clean and intuitive design can enhance the overall trading experience.

Liquidity is crucial for efficient trading. Choose exchanges with sufficient trading volume to ensure your orders can be executed promptly at fair prices.

Check if the exchange complies with regulatory standards in its operating jurisdictions. Regulated exchanges often prioritize user protection and adhere to legal requirements.

Stay informed about the latest news and updates related to your chosen exchange. Changes in policies, security measures, or supported assets can impact your trading strategy.

Regardless of the chosen exchange, implement the following security best practices to protect your assets:

Enable 2FA to add an extra layer of security to your account, requiring a secondary verification step for login.

Consider withdrawing your funds to a private wallet for long-term storage, especially for significant amounts of cryptocurrency.

Periodically update your exchange passwords to enhance security. Avoid using easily guessable passwords, and consider using a password manager.

Choosing the proper cryptocurrency exchange is akin to selecting the nexus where your financial aspirations converge with the dynamic world of digital assets. As you venture into the crypto cosmos, may your chosen exchange be the launchpad for transformative investments, propelling you towards realizing "CRYPTO RICH."

We will unravel advanced strategies, portfolio management techniques, and the nuances of specific trading styles. So, fasten your seatbelt as we navigate the complexities and opportunities within the ever-evolving landscape of cryptocurrency trading.

Security Measures in Crypto Investments

Transforming Investments into Crypto Millions," we navigate the intricacies of fortifying your financial fortress. Understanding and implementing robust security measures is not just a choice; it's necessary in the decentralized landscape where digital assets are the crown jewels.

The decentralized nature of cryptocurrencies empowers individuals with control over their financial assets. However, this empowerment comes with the responsibility of safeguarding one's holdings. Security measures in crypto investments are the shields that protect against the evolving threats of the digital frontier.

Let's explore a comprehensive set of security best practices to ensure the safety of your crypto investments.

Private keys are the gateway to your digital assets. Store them securely offline, preferably in hardware or paper wallets, to mitigate the risk of online threats.

Hardware wallets, such as Ledger or Trezor, provide an extra layer of security by keeping private keys offline. Use them for long-term storage of significant amounts of cryptocurrency.

Activate 2FA wherever possible, especially on exchanges and wallet accounts. This additional layer of verification significantly enhances security.

Keep your wallet software, exchange platforms, and other crypto-related applications current. Software updates often include security patches that protect against known vulnerabilities.

Exercise caution against phishing attempts. Verify URLs before accessing websites, avoid clicking on suspicious links, and be skeptical of unsolicited messages requesting personal information.

Distribute your investments across different wallets and exchanges. This strategy reduces the risk of a single point of failure affecting your entire portfolio.

Create regular backups of your wallet's private keys or recovery phrases. Store these backups in secure, offline locations to ensure access in unforeseen circumstances.

Avoid using public Wi-Fi to access your crypto accounts. Use a virtual private network (VPN) to secure your internet connection and encrypt data transmission when possible.

Additional security measures become crucial when dealing with cryptocurrency exchanges due to these platforms' centralized nature.

Before choosing an exchange, thoroughly research its security measures. Look for features like cold storage, regular security audits, and insurance coverage for potential losses.

After trading on an exchange, consider withdrawing your funds to a private wallet. This reduces the risk of exposure to potential security breaches on the exchange.

Keep a close eye on your exchange account activity. Set up alerts for significant transactions and regularly review your transaction history to detect unauthorized activity.

Some exchanges offer the option to allow withdrawal addresses. Enable this feature to ensure funds can only be withdrawn to pre-approved wallet addresses.

Stay informed about the regulatory landscape in your jurisdiction. Compliance with local laws and regulations adds a layer of protection and legitimacy to your crypto investments.

Ongoing education is a powerful weapon against potential security threats. Stay informed about the latest developments in crypto security, emerging threats, and best practices to adapt your security measures accordingly.

As we conclude this exploration of security measures in crypto investments, envision your journey as a shielded odyssey through the vast and sometimes treacherous crypto landscape. Implementing robust security practices protects your digital assets and contributes to the decentralized ecosystem's overall resilience.

4. Crypto Investment Strategies

Transforming Investments into Crypto Millions" unfolded as a tale of crypto alchemy—a narrative that transcended mere financial transactions and ventured into the art of investment strategies.

As the sun dipped below the digital skyline, Alex stood at the edge of a vast canvas, painted with the hues of blockchain possibilities. The crypto market, a dynamic masterpiece, beckoned with the promise of transformative wealth. But to navigate this realm required more than luck; it demanded the brushstroke precision of a seasoned artist.

In the opening notes of the crypto symphony, the HODLer's melody played—a timeless strategy that whispered tales of patience and long-term vision. Alex, a HODLer at heart, understood the power of holding onto digital assets through market storms. The strategy sang of weathering volatility, embracing the ebb and flow, and trusting in the inherent growth of the crypto ecosystem.

Yet, the canvas also displayed the lively dance of traders, and their moves were choreographed to the rhythm of market trends. Alex dipped their toes into the trader's waltz, exploring short-term maneuvers, swing trades, and trend-following strategies. The trader's art revealed itself in technical analysis, chart patterns, and swift decision-making—an intricate dance of risk and reward.

Venturing deeper into the canvas, Alex discovered the lush fields of yield farming—a form of crypto cultivation that redefined traditional notions of passive income. Like agricultural virtuosos, yield farmers sowed their assets in decentralized finance (DeFi) protocols, harvesting rewards and reaping the benefits of decentralized lending and liquidity provision.

As Alex donned the hat of a DeFi explorer, they journeyed through the uncharted territories of decentralized applications (DApps), liquidity pools, and governance tokens. The DeFi realm, a dynamic ecosystem of financial instruments, beckoned with the promise of decentralized exchanges, synthetic assets, and algorithmic stablecoins.

The canvas, however, was not limited to financial landscapes alone. Alex marveled at the vibrant strokes of non-fungible tokens (NFTs), each a unique masterpiece on the blockchain. Becoming a connoisseur of digital art, virtual real estate, and tokenized collectibles, Alex explored the world where creativity met blockchain, and rarity became a currency.

In this symphony of strategies, Alex recognized the importance of risk management—the maestro's baton that directed the harmony of their portfolio. Diversification, position sizing, and setting stop-loss orders became the tools to conduct a balanced and resilient investment orchestra.

As Alex's journey through the crypto canvas continued, they faced the dilemmas of the crypto alchemist. Each strategy, a unique potion of risk and reward, held the potential for financial transmutation. The challenge lay in finding the right blend, the perfect concoction aligned with their risk tolerance, financial goals, and the ever-evolving market conditions.

As the digital stars twinkled above, Alex stood at the intersection of crypto alchemy and personal artistry. Crafting their crypto opus required understanding the strategies and embracing the canvas's dynamic nature. The art of crypto investment strategies was a journey—a symphony where HODLing, trading, farming, exploring, and managing risk converged into a masterpiece that mirrored the spirit of "CRYPTO RICH."

She revealed the intricacies of managing a crypto portfolio, adapting to market shifts, and evolving as a crypto artist. Alex's journey continued a perpetual exploration of the boundless possibilities within the ever-changing crypto cosmos.

Long-Term vs. Short-Term Investments

Investors often need help with whether to adopt a long-term or short-term investment strategy. This chapter explores the nuances of these two approaches, shedding light on the considerations and potential outcomes associated with each.

Long-term investments, often synonymous with the HODLing strategy, involve holding onto assets for an extended period. This approach capitalizes on the potential for sustained growth and the fundamental strength of chosen assets. The allure lies in the resilience against short-term market fluctuations, with investors weathering volatility in anticipation of substantial returns over time.

Long-term investors, or HODLers, subscribe to a creed that emphasizes the fundamental value of chosen assets. The focus shifts from day-to-day market noise to the overarching potential of blockchain technology and decentralized finance. HODLing becomes a commitment to the transformative power of these technologies, requiring patience and a steadfast belief in the long-term viability of selected cryptocurrencies.

The journey of a long-term investor is challenging. Market corrections and bearish trends are opportunities to accumulate more of the chosen assets at favorable prices. The strategy involves navigating the seas of market volatility with resilience, looking beyond short-term fluctuations for long-term goals.

Contrastingly, short-term investments involve a more active approach to the market. Traders seek to capitalize on immediate opportunities, leveraging market volatility for quick gains. This strategy requires a keen understanding of market trends, technical analysis, and the ability to make agile decisions in response to changing conditions.

In the short term, investors develop the ability to read the market's pulse. Technical analysis becomes vital for making informed decisions based on price movements, chart patterns, and various market indicators. Success in short-term trading depends on quick thinking and strategic entry and exit points.

Recognizing the strengths of both long-term and short-term strategies, some investors adopt a hybrid approach. This involves maintaining a core portfolio of long-term holdings for stability and compounding potential while actively engaging in short-term trades to take advantage of market fluctuations. The hybrid approach seeks to balance the benefits of both worlds.

Regardless of the chosen strategy, effective risk management is crucial. Setting stop-loss orders, diversifying across assets, and aligning investment decisions with risk tolerance are fundamental principles applicable to both long-term and short-term approaches.

Investors often find themselves at the crossroads of long-term and short-term decisions. Creating a decision matrix that considers financial goals, risk appetite, prevailing market conditions, and the evolving crypto landscape helps guide strategic choices. Each decision becomes a part of the overall investment plan.

The distinction between long-term and short-term investments is not a rigid dichotomy but a dynamic tapestry of strategies. Investors navigate this landscape with an understanding that the choice between the two approaches is not absolute. Instead, it involves continuous adaptation to market conditions, strategic goals, and the evolving nature of the cryptocurrency space.

Risk Management in Cryptocurrency

The concept of diversification stands as a foundational strategy. Chapter 13 of "CRYPTO RICH: Transforming Investments into Crypto Millions" examines the dynamics of creating resilient crypto portfolios by spreading risks and capitalizing on opportunities.

Diversification serves as a fundamental principle in constructing a robust investment strategy. Its essence lies in mitigating risk by not relying excessively on a single asset. For investors like Alex, this principle is not just prudent; it is imperative in navigating the unpredictable nature of the crypto market.

At its core, diversification involves allocating investments across different assets to minimize the impact of poor performance in any one area. Alex perceives their portfolio as a diversified garden, recognizing that diversity is beneficial and essential for long-term growth and stability.

Diversification extends beyond the variety of cryptocurrencies in a portfolio. It encompasses different categories to achieve a well-rounded investment strategy:

We establish a foundation with well-established cryptocurrencies like Bitcoin and Ethereum for stability.

We are exploring alternative cryptocurrencies and tokens with unique use cases, balancing potential higher returns with increased volatility.

Venturing into the decentralized finance sector for opportunities in lending, liquidity provision, and yield farming while acknowledging associated risks.

We are integrating NFTs for exposure to the digital asset and collectibles market, recognizing the speculative nature of this segment.

Expanding the concept further, Alex considers geographical and sectoral diversification within the crypto space:

We are exploring opportunities across different geographical regions, considering regulatory environments, market trends, and emerging projects globally.

We are allocating investments across various sectors within the crypto space, such as blockchain infrastructure, decentralized applications, and emerging technologies.

In pursuing diversification, Alex acknowledges the delicate balance between risk and reward. While diversification minimizes risks, it introduces the challenge of optimizing the balance to maximize returns. This requires ongoing vigilance, research, and periodic portfolio reviews.

Amidst the enthusiasm for diversification, Alex remains aware of the potential downside of over-diversification. Diluting investments across too many assets can mitigate the impact of successful ones and hinder the potential for significant gains. Alex emphasizes the importance of quality over quantity, ensuring each asset aligns with the overall portfolio strategy.

Understanding the evolving nature of market dynamics, Alex emphasizes the significance of tactical rebalancing. Regularly reassessing the portfolio allows for adjustments based on market conditions, changing trends, and the achievement of strategic goals.

As this chapter concludes, Alex envisions their crypto portfolio as a mosaic—a carefully curated composition of diverse elements. Diversification is not a one-time effort but an ongoing, adaptive process, a strategic masterpiece that evolves with the dynamic crypto landscape.

Alex's journey through the crypto cosmos will unfold, exploring advanced strategies, risk management techniques, and the intricacies of optimizing a diversified portfolio. The art of diversification, a cornerstone in the pursuit of becoming "CRYPTO RICH," reflects strategic understanding and resilience in the face of market uncertainties.

Risk Management in Cryptocurrency

Transforming Investments into Crypto Millions" delves into the crucial aspect of risk management. This chapter explores the methodologies and strategies employed by prudent investors to navigate uncertainties and safeguard their portfolios in the dynamic world of cryptocurrency.

Risk in cryptocurrency is an inherent facet of the market's volatility and susceptibility to various factors. Recognizing this, investors manage comprehensive risk to mitigate potential downsides and protect their capital.
Diversifying investments across different cryptocurrencies, asset classes, and sectors is a fundamental strategy. By spreading risk,

investors aim to reduce the impact of poor performance in any area.

Prudent investors carefully determine the size of each position within their portfolio. This involves allocating a specific percentage of the total capital to individual assets, preventing overexposure to any single investment.

Setting Stop-Loss Orders

Transforming Investments into Crypto Millions" explores the vital practice of setting stop-loss orders in the dynamic world of cryptocurrency. In this chapter, we delve into the strategic considerations, benefits, and best practices that underpin the use of stop-loss orders as a robust risk management tool.

Setting a stop-loss order is akin to placing a safety net beneath the tightrope of cryptocurrency investment. It is a predetermined sell order that automatically executes when an asset's price reaches a specified level. This strategic tool limits potential losses and protects investors from unforeseen market downturns.

The primary goal of a stop-loss order is to mitigate risk. Investors establish a precise risk tolerance level by defining an exit point before entering a trade. This ensures that losses are contained within predetermined parameters, preventing emotional decision-making during market turbulence.

Setting stop-loss orders enforces discipline in investment strategies. It removes the emotional aspect of decision-making during market volatility, preventing investors from succumbing to fear or greed. It acts as a predetermined plan, allowing for rational decision-making despite unexpected price movements.

Investors often employ technical analysis to identify key support levels, trendlines, or moving averages as potential stop-loss levels.

These technical indicators help in setting levels that align with the asset's historical price movements.

Volatility plays a crucial role in determining stop-loss levels. More volatile assets may require wider stop-loss margins to account for natural price fluctuations, while less volatile assets may have tighter stop-loss parameters.

The stop-loss level should also consider the broader portfolio context. Investors may set different stop-loss levels based on the risk associated with specific assets and their overall portfolio strategy.

A market order is triggered immediately when the asset's price reaches the specified stop-loss level. While providing swift execution, market orders may face slippage during highly volatile periods.

Limit orders are executed only at the specified price or better. This provides more control over the execution price but may result in the order needing to be filled if the market moves swiftly.

Setting stop-loss orders is not a one-time task; it requires ongoing monitoring and adjustment. Investors should regularly reassess market conditions, news developments, and overall portfolio performance to ensure that stop-loss levels align with their risk tolerance and investment goals.

Setting stop-loss orders is a powerful practice that empowers investors to navigate the volatile waters of cryptocurrency markets with greater confidence and control. It is both an art and a science—a strategic tool that, when wielded effectively, adds a layer of protection to investment portfolios.

The narrative will continue to explore advanced strategies, emerging trends, and the evolving landscape of cryptocurrency. The art of setting stop-loss orders remains a cornerstone in the journey toward financial prosperity and resilience in the crypto realm.

This chapter explores the methodologies, tools, and insights that investors employ to make informed decisions in the dynamic and ever-evolving cryptocurrency markets.

Understanding the intricacies of the crypto market is a foundational step for any investor seeking success. Market research is not merely a choice but an essential component of strategic decision-making, providing a roadmap through the complexities of the digital asset landscape.

Fundamental analysis involves evaluating the intrinsic value of a cryptocurrency by examining factors such as technology, team expertise, use cases, partnerships, and overall project viability. This method forms the bedrock of comprehensive market research, allowing investors to gauge the long-term potential of a digital asset.

Technical analysis focuses on studying historical price movements and trading volumes to predict future price trends. Investors use charts, indicators, and patterns to identify potential entry and exit points, providing a more tactical perspective on market movements.

Sentiment analysis involves gauging market sentiment through social media, news, and community forums. Understanding the market's collective mood can offer insights into potential price movements and overall market direction.
Exchanges serve as primary platforms for trading and are valuable sources of real-time market data. Investors leverage features such

as order books, price charts, and trading volumes to inform their decisions.

Blockchain explorers provide transparency into the transaction history of cryptocurrencies. They allow investors to track transactions, monitor wallet balances, and verify the authenticity of on-chain activities.

Staying informed about industry news is crucial. News aggregators compile information from various sources, keeping investors updated on market developments, regulatory changes, and project updates.

Investors conduct in-depth research on individual projects, examining whitepapers, development progress, and community engagement. This approach is essential for understanding the unique features and potential risks associated with each cryptocurrency.

Macro market analysis involves studying broader market trends, including overall market capitalization, dominance of specific cryptocurrencies, and prevailing sentiment. This approach helps investors position themselves strategically within the larger market context.

Understanding the regulatory environment in various jurisdictions is crucial. Changes in regulations can significantly impact the value and legality of specific cryptocurrencies.

Investors must prioritize the security features of cryptocurrencies, wallets, and exchanges. A robust security infrastructure is essential for safeguarding assets from potential cyber threats. Market research is not a static process; it requires continuous learning and adaptation. Successful investors stay informed about emerging technologies, market trends, and potential risks, ensuring their strategies remain dynamic and relevant.

It becomes evident that crypto market research is both a science and an art—a strategic endeavor that empowers investors to make informed decisions in the ever-evolving cryptocurrency landscape. In the chapters, the narrative will continue to explore advanced strategies, risk management techniques, and the evolving trends shaping the journey toward financial prosperity in the crypto realm. Awareness of and compliance with regulatory requirements in various jurisdictions is crucial. Regulatory landscape changes can significantly impact the value and viability of specific cryptocurrencies.

Understanding the security features of chosen cryptocurrencies, wallets, and exchanges is vital. Knowledgeable investors take measures to protect their assets from potential cybersecurity threats.

Recognizing that market conditions evolve, successful investors engage in dynamic risk management. This involves continuous reassessment of the portfolio adjusting strategies based on changing trends, news, and overall market sentiment.

When transforming investments into crypto millions, it" delves into risk mitigation through insurance and hedging strategies in the cryptocurrency market. This chapter explores the innovative methods investors employ to protect their wealth against unforeseen events and market volatility.

As the cryptocurrency market matures, investors recognize the importance of safeguarding their assets against various risks, from market fluctuations to operational vulnerabilities. Insurance and hedging strategies emerge as valuable tools to mitigate potential losses and protect portfolios.

Some platforms and custodians offer insurance coverage for digital assets held on their platforms. This protects against potential hacks, theft, or other security breaches.

Intelligent contract insurance has gained prominence with the rise of decentralized finance (DeFi) applications. Insurance protocols within the DeFi space offer coverage against vulnerabilities and exploits in intelligent contracts.

Options contracts provide investors the right, but not the obligation, to buy or sell an asset at a predetermined price. Investors can use options to hedge against potential losses or generate income while managing risk.

Futures contracts allow investors to lock in the price of an asset at a future date. This hedging tool enables participants to protect themselves from adverse price movements.

The DeFi space has witnessed the emergence of decentralized insurance platforms that operate on blockchain technology. These platforms use smart contracts to facilitate peer-to-peer insurance coverage against various risks.

In decentralized liquidity pools, where users contribute funds for trading and lending, insurance protocols offer coverage against impermanent loss and other risks associated with providing liquidity.

The developing nature of the crypto insurance industry presents challenges related to the need for regulatory frameworks. Investors must carefully assess the credibility and legitimacy of insurance providers.
Options and futures trading involve complexity that may be daunting for some investors. A thorough understanding of these instruments is essential to leverage them effectively.

Investors tailor their hedging strategies to align with their investment goals and risk tolerance. Whether using options, futures, or decentralized insurance, the approach must complement the broader portfolio strategy.

Strategically allocating insured assets within a diversified portfolio enhances risk mitigation. Investors balance risk exposure by identifying critical areas where insurance and hedging strategies can be most effective.

In conclusion, exploring crypto insurance and hedging strategies underscores the evolving nature of risk management in the cryptocurrency market. As the industry matures, these innovative tools allow investors to balance risk and reward, safeguarding their wealth in an unpredictable financial landscape.

The art of risk mitigation remains a cornerstone in the journey toward financial prosperity and resilience in the crypto realm. Managing risk in cryptocurrency extends beyond technical strategies; it involves cultivating psychological resilience. The ability to withstand market fluctuations, avoid impulsive decisions, and maintain a disciplined approach contributes significantly to long-term success.

Ongoing education is a fundamental component of effective risk management. Investors stay abreast of industry developments, emerging technologies, and potential risks to make informed decisions.

As the chapter concludes, it becomes evident that risk management in cryptocurrency is a multifaceted discipline. Successful investors navigate the crypto seas with strategic planning, adaptability, and a keen understanding of the market forces.

The art of risk management remains an integral part of the journey toward financial prosperity in the crypto realm.

5. Identifying Promising Cryptocurrencies

Transforming Investments into Crypto Millions" unravels a narrative woven with the anticipation and excitement of discovering the following promising cryptocurrencies. Our protagonist, Morgan, a diligent investor, embarks on a journey into research, intuition, and strategic insight.

A seasoned investor, Morgan understands that the crypto market is more than just Bitcoin and Ethereum. It's a vast universe filled with hidden gems—cryptocurrencies with untapped potential waiting to be unearthed. The allure of these hidden gems lies in the possibility of substantial returns and groundbreaking innovations.

Armed with a curious spirit and a laptop, Morgan delves into the world of promising cryptocurrencies. The research journey begins with a quest for information, exploring various sources:

The heart of any cryptocurrency project lies in its whitepaper. Morgan meticulously reads through these documents, seeking to understand each project's technology, use case, and vision. The whitepaper becomes a treasure map, guiding Morgan through the intricacies of promising ventures.

Behind every promising cryptocurrency is a dedicated team. Morgan scrutinizes the backgrounds, experiences, and accomplishments of the project's founders and developers. A solid and capable team often serves as a beacon of reliability and competence.

Morgan recognizes the importance of community support. Active and engaged communities signify a solid user base and a network of passionate advocates who believe in the project. Social media platforms and community forums become valuable landscapes for gauging sentiment.

As Morgan navigates the vast sea of cryptocurrencies, technological innovation emerges as a crucial criterion. Morgan explores projects that introduce novel concepts, improve scalability, or address existing challenges uniquely. The potential for groundbreaking technology often sets promising cryptocurrencies apart.

Understanding the market potential of a cryptocurrency is a strategic move. Morgan analyzes factors such as:

How well does the cryptocurrency address a specific market need? Morgan evaluates whether the project has a clear use case and a target audience.

Strategic partnerships and collaborations can be indicative of a cryptocurrency's potential. Morgan investigates whether the project has established connections with reputable organizations and other blockchain projects.

Morgan is aware that the pursuit of promising cryptocurrencies carries inherent risks. Risk management becomes an integral part of the journey, and Morgan carefully evaluates factors such as:

Morgan assesses whether the project has a realistic roadmap and a clear path to implementation. Ambitious goals are welcomed, but feasibility is paramount.

Understanding the regulatory landscape is crucial. Morgan seeks projects that demonstrate an awareness of and adherence to regulatory requirements, reducing the risk of legal complications.

Beyond the metrics and data, Morgan acknowledges the role of intuition and timing. Recognizing that the crypto market is influenced by trends, sentiment, and external factors, Morgan relies on a gut feeling honed through experience.

The allure of hidden gems, the diligence of research, and the intuition cultivated through experience propel Morgan forward. In the chapters to come, the narrative will unfold further, revealing the challenges, triumphs, and strategic decisions that shape Morgan's crypto odyssey in the quest for financial prosperity and wealth in the crypto realm.

Researching and Analyzing Projects

Understanding the intricacies of blockchain is paramount when researching and analyzing projects. This chapter delves into the fundamental aspects of blockchain technology, exploring its significance and impact on identifying promising cryptocurrency projects.

Decentralization is a crucial feature of blockchain technology. Analyze how the project leverages decentralization to enhance security, transparency, and resilience. Projects with a robust decentralization model are often more resistant to censorship and single points of failure.

Explore the consensus mechanism employed by the blockchain. Whether Proof of Work (PoW), Proof of Stake (PoS), or another model, each has its strengths and weaknesses. Assess the chosen consensus mechanism's efficiency, security, and environmental impact.

Examine the implementation of smart contracts within the blockchain. Smart contracts enable self-executing agreements, automating processes and reducing the need for intermediaries. Evaluate how well the project utilizes intelligent contracts to create real-world applications.

Scalability is a critical factor for the success of any blockchain project. Investigate the scalability solutions employed, such as sharding or layer-two solutions. Assess the project's ability to handle a growing user base without compromising performance.

Analyze the transaction speed and throughput of the blockchain. A high-performance blockchain facilitates quicker and more cost-effective transactions, contributing to a better user experience. Consider how the project addresses scalability challenges to maintain optimal performance.

Evaluate the project's approach to interoperability. Blockchain interoperability allows different blockchains to communicate and share information seamlessly. Projects that embrace interoperability are often better positioned for integration into broader ecosystems.

Assess the privacy and security features implemented within the blockchain. Privacy-centric cryptocurrencies often incorporate advanced cryptographic techniques to protect user data. Strong security measures are vital for building trust and reliability in the ecosystem.

Examine the token standards supported by the blockchain. Customizable tokens allow various applications, from simple transfers to complex programmable assets. Projects that offer flexibility in token creation cater to diverse use cases.

Explore how the project integrates or plans to integrate AI into its blockchain ecosystem. AI can enhance security, automate decision-making processes, and improve overall efficiency.

Assess the compatibility of the blockchain with IoT devices. The intersection of blockchain and IoT can create new possibilities, particularly in supply chain management, logistics, and data integrity.

Investigate how the blockchain implements upgrades and improvements. A dynamic and adaptable project will likely remain relevant as technology evolves. Assess the project's upgrade mechanisms and the community's involvement in the decision-making process.

Analyze the governance model of the blockchain. Governance structures determine how decisions are made within the ecosystem. Evaluate whether the governance model is decentralized, inclusive, and capable of addressing conflicts effectively.

A deep understanding of its core components and the project's commitment to scalability, security, and innovation is essential when researching and analyzing potential investments. As the crypto landscape matures, projects prioritizing and leveraging blockchain advancements will likely stand out as promising and enduring contributors to the digital economy.

While blockchain technology lays the foundation for cryptocurrency projects, the human element is equally crucial. The team behind a project, their experience, and their ability to navigate the complexities of the crypto space play a pivotal role in its success. This chapter explores the significance of team and development expertise when researching and analyzing cryptocurrency projects.

Examine the composition of the project's team. A diverse and multidisciplinary team often brings a range of skills and perspectives. Look for a balance of technical expertise, business acumen, and industry experience within the team.

Assess the leadership qualities of crucial team members. Effective leadership fosters innovation, decision-making, and adaptability. Investigate how leaders have handled challenges in the past and their vision for the project's future.

Evaluate the team's experience with blockchain technology. Previous involvement in successful blockchain projects or contributions to the broader blockchain community can indicate a solid understanding of the complexities and challenges unique to the space.

Assess the coding and development skills within the team. A proficient development team is essential for implementing and maintaining the technical aspects of the project. Review the team's GitHub activity and contributions to open-source projects.

Investigate the team's experience in the cryptocurrency and related industries. Relevant industry experience can provide insights into the team's understanding of market dynamics, regulatory challenges, and user needs.

Examine the success of the team's previous projects. A track record of delivering successful and innovative projects is a positive indicator of the team's capability to execute and bring value to their current endeavor.

Evaluate the team's communication style. Transparent and open communication fosters trust within the community. Assess how effectively the team communicates updates, challenges, and plans to their audience.

Assess the level of community engagement demonstrated by the team. A team that actively engages with its community listens to feedback, and addresses concerns indicates a commitment to building a supportive and involved user base.

Examine how the team has handled challenges and setbacks. Adapting to changing circumstances and navigating obstacles is crucial in the dynamic and often unpredictable crypto landscape.

Evaluate how the team responds to feedback from the community. A team that listens to its users and iterates on its product based on feedback demonstrates a commitment to continuous improvement.

The team behind a cryptocurrency project is the driving force that transforms vision into reality. Investors can gain valuable insights into the project's potential success by carefully analyzing the team's composition, technical proficiency, track record, transparency, and adaptability. In the rapidly evolving world of cryptocurrency, where challenges and opportunities abound, a solid and capable team is a cornerstone for building sustainable and impactful projects.

Beyond the intricacies of blockchain technology and the prowess of development teams, the real-world application and use case of a cryptocurrency project are integral factors in determining its potential for success. This chapter explores the importance of use cases and practical applications when researching and analyzing cryptocurrency projects.

Examine the cryptocurrency project's use case and ability to address real-world problems. Projects that aim to solve tangible issues or improve existing processes are often more likely to gain adoption and long-term value.

Evaluate the relevance of the project's use case within its target market. A well-defined use case that aligns with market demands is crucial for attracting users, partners, and investors.

Analyze the user experience offered by the project. A user-friendly interface and seamless integration into existing workflows contribute to the practical application of cryptocurrency.

Assess the potential for widespread adoption within the intended user base. Projects with a clear and compelling use case are more likely to gain traction and become valuable contributors to their respective industries.

Explore the disruptive potential of the cryptocurrency project within its industry. Assess how the project's use case challenges traditional models and whether it introduces innovative solutions.

Examine the project's ability to form partnerships and collaborations within its industry. Strong partnerships can amplify the project's impact and contribute to its real-world application.

Evaluate the usefulness of the project's native token within its ecosystem. A token with straightforward utility and a defined role in facilitating transactions, governance, or other functions enhances the project's practical application.

Assess the economic model that governs the project's tokenomics. A well-balanced economic model contributes to the stability and sustainability of the cryptocurrency's value, supporting its real-world application.

Investigate the project's compliance with regulatory standards in its target markets. Projects that navigate regulatory challenges effectively are better positioned for real-world adoption and long-term success.

Assess the legal framework surrounding the project and its industry. A clear understanding of legal considerations ensures the project's longevity and legitimacy.

The real-world application and use case of a cryptocurrency project are essential components in determining its potential for success. As the crypto landscape evolves, projects that address tangible problems, provide practical value and navigate regulatory challenges effectively are more likely to stand the test of time. When researching and analyzing cryptocurrency projects, a keen focus on use cases and practical applications ensures a comprehensive evaluation of their potential impact on industries and communities.

Understanding and interpreting market trends and the regulatory environment is essential for effectively researching and analyzing cryptocurrency projects. This chapter explores the dynamic interplay between market trends and regulatory factors and their influence on the potential success of blockchain-based initiatives.

Explore the prevailing trend of tokenization and the rise of digital assets. Assess how the project aligns with or contributes to this trend, indicating its relevance and adaptability to the evolving crypto landscape.

Examine the growth of decentralized finance (DeFi) and the associated trend of yield farming. Projects that integrate or contribute to the DeFi ecosystem may have increased appeal due to the growing interest in decentralized financial services.

Understand the global regulatory framework for cryptocurrencies. Assess how the project complies with existing regulations and anticipates changes in different jurisdictions. Regulatory adherence is crucial for mitigating legal risks.

Analyze the level of acceptance and recognition of cryptocurrencies by governments. Projects operating in jurisdictions with a positive stance toward digital assets may experience fewer regulatory hurdles and increased market opportunities.

Investigate the project's compliance with Anti-Money Laundering (AML) and Know Your Customer (KYC) regulations. A commitment to robust compliance measures enhances the project's legitimacy and reduces the risk of legal challenges.

Assess the governance framework of the project. Transparent and effective governance structures demonstrate the project's commitment to regulatory compliance and responsible management.

Analyze the historical performance of the project's native token. Track price movements, trading volume, and market capitalization. Historical data provides insights into the market perception and potential future trends.

Evaluate adoption metrics, including the number of users, transactions, and network activity. Increasing adoption is often a positive sign of a project's viability and acceptance within the broader market.

Explore the integration of Non-Fungible Tokens (NFTs) within the project. The NFT trend has gained significant traction, and projects incorporating NFTs may attract a broader user base and community.

Assess the project's approach to cross-chain compatibility. With the rise of interoperability, projects that can seamlessly interact with other blockchains may have a strategic advantage in the market.

Market trends and the regulatory environment are pivotal factors in researching and analyzing cryptocurrency projects. A comprehensive understanding of emerging trends, global regulatory frameworks, and the project's compliance measures is essential for making informed investment decisions. By navigating the dynamic landscape of market trends and regulatory requirements, investors can position themselves to identify projects that not only adapt to change but also contribute meaningfully to the evolving crypto ecosystem.

Fundamental Analysis of Cryptocurrencies

Chapter 12: Security and Technology: Safeguarding the Foundations of Cryptocurrencies

This chapter explores the critical role of security and technology in fundamental analysis, providing insights into how these aspects contribute to cryptocurrencies' overall robustness and long-term viability.

Examine the cryptographic foundations of the cryptocurrency. A solid and well-implemented cryptographic framework ensures the security of transactions, addresses privacy concerns, and protects user data.

Evaluate the consensus mechanism employed by the cryptocurrency. Whether Proof of Work (PoW), Proof of Stake (PoS), or another model, the chosen consensus mechanism impacts security, decentralization, and attack resistance.

Assess the overall security of the blockchain network. Investigate the measures to prevent double-spending, 51% attacks, and other vulnerabilities. A secure network is essential for maintaining user trust and avoiding malicious activities.

Explore the scalability solutions implemented by the cryptocurrency. Scalability is crucial for handling increased transaction volumes and ensuring the smooth functioning of the network. Projects that address scalability effectively are better positioned for widespread adoption.

Assess the implementation of smart contracts and decentralized applications (DApps) within the ecosystem. Smart contracts enable self-executing agreements, and a thriving ecosystem of DApps indicates practical application and innovation within the project.

Evaluate the interoperability of the cryptocurrency with other blockchains. Interoperability enhances the project's flexibility and allows it to collaborate seamlessly with other projects, contributing to a more interconnected blockchain ecosystem.

Investigate whether the cryptocurrency has undergone third-party security audits. External audits conducted by reputable firms provide additional assurance regarding the project's security measures.

Examine the open-source nature of the project's code. Projects with transparent, open-source code allow the community to review, contribute, and identify potential vulnerabilities, fostering a collaborative approach to security.

Evaluate the project's incident response plan. A well-defined plan demonstrates the team's preparedness to handle security incidents promptly and effectively, minimizing potential damage and maintaining user confidence.

Investigate the project's history with security incidents. Assess how the team has handled previous challenges, the lessons learned, and the measures implemented to prevent similar incidents in the future.

Examine the project's long-term technological roadmap. A clear and ambitious roadmap demonstrates the team's commitment to continuous improvement, innovation, and adapting to evolving industry standards.

Assess how the project approaches software upgrades and forks. A well-managed upgrade process ensures that the project remains secure, competitive, and aligned with the evolving needs of the cryptocurrency ecosystem.

Security and technology are fundamental pillars in the evaluation of cryptocurrencies. By delving into the cryptographic foundations, consensus mechanisms, technological innovations, code transparency, and the project's response to security incidents, investors can understand a cryptocurrency's strength and resilience. In a space where trust is paramount, projects prioritizing and continually investing in robust security measures and technological advancements are more likely to emerge as promising and enduring contributors to digital assets.

Regulatory compliance plays a pivotal role in the fundamental analysis of cryptocurrencies. As the cryptocurrency landscape evolves, understanding how projects adhere to and navigate regulatory frameworks becomes crucial for assessing their long-term viability and minimizing legal risks. This chapter explores the significance of regulatory compliance and its impact on identifying promising cryptocurrencies.

Examine the project's approach to regulatory compliance in various jurisdictions. Cryptocurrencies often face different regulatory challenges in other countries, and projects that proactively address these variances demonstrate a commitment to navigating the global regulatory landscape.

Assess the level of regulatory clarity in the jurisdictions where the project operates. Clear and well-defined regulations provide a stable environment for cryptocurrency projects to thrive and attract users and investors.

Investigate the project's Anti-Money Laundering (AML) and Know Your Customer (KYC) policies. Robust and compliant AML and KYC measures contribute to the project's legitimacy and mitigate the risk of illicit activities.

Examine the project's approach to user privacy. While regulatory compliance is essential, projects prioritizing user privacy and data protection are committed to ethical practices.

Evaluate the project's engagement with regulatory bodies. Projects that proactively collaborate with regulators, seeking guidance and establishing open communication channels, are better positioned to adapt to evolving regulatory requirements.

Assess whether the project has legal counsel specializing in blockchain and cryptocurrency regulations. Legal expertise is crucial for navigating complex regulatory landscapes and ensuring the project remains compliant.

Determine the regulatory classification of the project's native token. Understanding whether the token is classified as a security or utility token is essential for complying with securities regulations and offering clarity to investors.

Investigate the project's compliance with securities laws, primarily if the native token is classified as a security. Adherence to securities regulations is vital for avoiding legal complications and maintaining trust within the investor community.

Examine the project's history with regulatory incidents. Assess how the team has handled past regulatory challenges, the lessons learned, and the measures implemented to prevent similar incidents in the future.

Consider the impact of regulatory compliance on the project's reputation. A positive reputation for regulatory adherence can enhance the project's credibility, attract institutional investors, and foster a positive community perception.

Stay informed about ongoing regulatory developments. Understand how the project adapts to regulatory updates and positions itself to comply with emerging standards, demonstrating a commitment to future preparedness.

Assess the project's ability to forecast and adapt to potential regulatory changes. A forward-thinking approach to regulatory compliance is essential for navigating the uncertainties of the evolving legal landscape.

As the industry matures, projects prioritizing and navigating the complex regulatory environment effectively are more likely to establish themselves as trustworthy, compliant, and enduring contributors to the broader financial ecosystem. Investors should consider regulatory adherence as a foundational element when evaluating the long-term potential of cryptocurrencies and blockchain projects.

Technical Analysis for Crypto Investments

The significance of candlestick patterns and the overall chart analysis environment, providing insights into how these tools can illuminate potential trends, reversals, and market sentiment for crypto investors engaged in technical analysis.

Start with the fundamentals of candlestick construction. Explain how each candlestick represents a specific time frame and includes elements such as the body, wick, and tail. Illustrate the meaning of a bullish and bearish candle.

Introduce common candlestick patterns and their interpretations. Discuss patterns like Doji, Hammer, Shooting Star, Engulfing Patterns, and more. Explain how recognizing these patterns can provide insights into potential market movements.

Discuss the importance of selecting appropriate time frames for chart analysis. Explore the differences between short-term and long-term time frames and how they can impact the accuracy of predictions.

Explain the process of trend identification using trendlines. Showcase how drawing trendlines on a chart can help investors visualize and understand the prevailing market trends, supporting decision-making.

Explore how candlestick patterns can indicate trend reversals or continuations. Provide real-world examples of how identifying these patterns has assisted traders in predicting market movements.

Illustrate how candlestick patterns can be used to confirm support and resistance levels. Discuss scenarios where specific candlestick patterns align with key levels, providing additional confirmation for traders.

Introduce the concept of multiple time frame analysis. Discuss how analyzing charts across different time frames can provide a more comprehensive understanding of market trends and potential entry or exit points.

Explore the role of trading volume in confirming or contradicting candlestick patterns. Discuss how changes in volume can strengthen or weaken the signals provided by candlestick patterns.

Discuss the availability of advanced charting tools and features on cryptocurrency trading platforms. Highlight how these tools can enhance the efficiency of chart analysis and pattern recognition.

Introduce the concept of automated trading strategies based on candlestick patterns. Discuss the use of algorithms and bots that leverage chart analysis to execute trades automatically.

Explore how candlestick patterns reflect market sentiment. Discuss the psychological factors contributing to forming specific patterns and their implications for investor behavior.

Highlight the emotional aspect of trading and the importance of risk management. Discuss how understanding chart patterns can help investors make more rational decisions and manage risks effectively.

Candlestick patterns and chart analysis create a visual language savvy crypto investors can interpret to make informed decisions. By understanding the nuances of these patterns and the broader chart analysis environment, investors can gain insights into market dynamics, identify potential opportunities, and navigate the complexities of the cryptocurrency landscape with greater confidence. However, it's crucial to remember that no analysis tool is foolproof, and a comprehensive investment strategy should incorporate a blend of technical analysis, fundamental analysis, and prudent risk management.

Indicators and oscillators are:
- Potent tools in the technical analyst's toolkit.
- Offering insights into market trends.
- Momentum.
- Potential reversals.
-

This chapter explores the dynamic environment of indicators and oscillators within crypto investments, providing a comprehensive guide for investors seeking to navigate and interpret these essential tools.

Introduce the concept of moving averages and their significance in trend analysis. Discuss the types of moving averages (simple, exponential) and how they can smooth out price data to reveal underlying trends.

Explore the RSI as a momentum oscillator. Explain how RSI measures the speed and change of price movements, indicating overbought or oversold conditions. Discuss common RSI strategies for crypto investors.

Explain the components of the MACD indicator, including the MACD line, signal line, and histogram. Discuss how MACD reveals changes in a trend's strength, direction, momentum, and duration. Explore the significance of signal line crossovers and MACD histogram divergences. Discuss how these events signal potential buy or sell opportunities and provide insights into trend reversals. Introduce the stochastic oscillator as a momentum indicator.

Discuss the calculation of %K and %D lines and how they identify overbought or oversold conditions.
Discuss how traders use signal confirmation and divergences in the stochastic oscillator to make trading decisions. Explain how this oscillator can be a valuable tool in assessing market momentum.

Explain the construction of Bollinger Bands using a simple moving average and standard deviations. Discuss how Bollinger Bands reveal volatility and potential price reversals.
Explore the concept of the Bollinger Bands squeeze and expansion. Discuss how traders interpret these events to anticipate potential breakout or breakdown situations.
Discuss the benefits and challenges of combining multiple indicators and oscillators. Explore how traders use a holistic approach to technical analysis by integrating insights from various tools.

Explore the use of algorithms in trading strategies that incorporate indicators. Discuss how automated trading systems leverage indicators to make data-driven decisions.
Highlight the unique challenges and opportunities presented by the inherent volatility of the cryptocurrency market. Discuss how indicators and oscillators can be adapted to analyze crypto price movements effectively.

Emphasize the importance of risk management strategies when trading cryptocurrencies, especially when using indicators and oscillators. Discuss how to set appropriate stop-loss orders and manage position sizes.

Indicators and oscillators are critical to the technical analyst's arsenal, offering valuable insights into market dynamics. By understanding the nuances of these tools, crypto investors can make informed decisions, identify potential entry and exit points, and navigate the complexities of the dynamic cryptocurrency environment. However, it's crucial to approach technical analysis with a well-rounded perspective, combining insights from fundamental analysis, risk management, and an understanding of broader market trends.

Volume is a powerful indicator in technical analysis, offering crucial insights into the strength and sustainability of price movements. Understanding volume analysis is essential for gaining a comprehensive view of market dynamics in cryptocurrency investments. This chapter explores the significance of volume analysis and its application in making informed decisions within the crypto space.

Define trading volume and its representation in price charts. Explain how volume reflects the number of assets traded during a specific period and measures market activity.

Explore how volume bars are represented on price charts. Discuss the implications of different volume patterns, such as spikes, surges, and periods of low volume, and their relevance to market trends.

Explain how increasing volume can confirm the strength of an existing trend. Discuss scenarios where rising volume aligns with upward or downward price movements, reinforcing the likelihood of a trend continuation.

Explore the concept of volume divergence as a potential signal for trend reversals. Discuss how decreasing volume during an uptrend or downtrend may indicate weakening momentum and the possibility of a reversal.

Discuss how volume analysis can confirm the validity of price breakouts. Explore scenarios where high volume accompanies a breakout, validating the likelihood of a sustained price movement.

Explore the concept of volume climax and exhaustion. Discuss how extremely high volume, often accompanied by significant price changes, may signal a potential climax in buying or selling activity, indicating a reversal.

Introduce the On-Balance-Volume (OBV) indicator to incorporate volume into traditional price charts. Discuss how OBV accumulates or distributes volume based on price movements.

Explore how traders use OBV to identify divergence and confirmation signals. Discuss scenarios where OBV divergence may precede price reversals or where rising OBV confirms an uptrend.

Discuss how bullish and bearish volume analysis can provide insights into market sentiment. Explore scenarios where an increase in bullish volume supports optimism, while an increase in bearish volume may signal caution.

Introduce the Fear and Greed Index as a sentiment indicator considering various factors, including volume. Discuss how extreme fear or greed, often reflected in trading volume, may signal potential market reversals.

Highlight the availability of advanced volume analytics on cryptocurrency trading platforms. Discuss how these tools can assist investors in analyzing volume patterns and making informed trading decisions.

Introduce the concepts of Volume Profile and Market Depth as advanced tools for volume analysis. Discuss how these tools provide a more nuanced understanding of market volume distribution and order flow.

Volume analysis is a crucial component of technical analysis in cryptocurrency investments. By deciphering the patterns and signals embedded in trading volume, investors can enhance their understanding of market dynamics, confirm trend strength, and identify potential reversal points. However, it's essential to integrate volume analysis with other technical indicators and fundamental analysis for a comprehensive approach to decision-making. In the dynamic and rapidly evolving crypto market, volume analysis is valuable for those seeking to navigate the complexities and capitalize on opportunities.

Trend analysis and trendlines are fundamental aspects of technical analysis, providing investors valuable insights into market direction and potential entry or exit points. Understanding how to identify, confirm, and trade trends is crucial for making informed decisions in cryptocurrency investments. This chapter explores the significance of trend analysis and the application of trendlines in the dynamic crypto market.

Define what constitutes a trend in the context of cryptocurrency markets. Discuss the concepts of uptrends, downtrends, and sideways trends, emphasizing the importance of trend identification in technical analysis.

Explain the duration of trends and their different phases, such as the accumulation, uptrend, distribution, and downtrend. Discuss how understanding these phases can aid in anticipating market movements.

Explore common price patterns that signify trends, including higher highs and higher lows in an uptrend and lower highs and lower lows in a downtrend. Discuss how recognizing these patterns can be the foundation of trend analysis.

Discuss the role of moving averages in identifying trends. Explore how moving averages smooth out price data, making it easier to identify the market's overall direction.

Explain the process of drawing trendlines on price charts. Discuss the significance of connecting consecutive highs or lows to form trendlines and how they act as visual guides for trend analysis.

Discuss different types of trendlines, including support and resistance trendlines. Explore how support trendlines connect consecutive lows and act as potential buying zones while resistance trendlines converge consecutive highs as potential selling zones.

Emphasize the importance of multiple touchpoints for confirming the validity of trendlines. Discuss how trendlines with more touches are considered more robust and reliable indicators of trend direction.

Explore how trendline breakouts or violations can signal potential trend reversals. Discuss the significance of analyzing volume and other indicators to confirm trendline breakouts.

Introduce the concept of trend channels formed by parallel trendlines. Discuss how these channels can visually represent the price range within an established trend.

Discuss trading strategies within trend channels, including identifying potential entry and exit points. Explore how trend channels can help investors set realistic price targets and manage risk.

Introduce Fibonacci retracements and extensions as tools for advanced trend analysis. Discuss how Fibonacci levels can be used to identify potential reversal zones and extensions to project future price targets.

Explore the benefits of applying trend analysis across multiple time frames. Discuss how aligning trends on shorter and longer time frames can provide a more comprehensive view of market dynamics.

Highlight the availability of advanced charting software on cryptocurrency trading platforms. Discuss how these tools offer features such as drawing tools, trendline customization, and trend analysis indicators.

Discuss how algorithmic trading strategies often incorporate trend analysis. Explore how automated trading systems use trendlines and other indicators to make data-driven decisions.

Trend analysis and trendlines are indispensable tools for crypto investors seeking to navigate market trends and make informed trading decisions. By mastering the art of identifying trends, drawing trendlines, and incorporating advanced techniques, investors can enhance their ability to spot opportunities, manage risk, and thrive in the dynamic landscape of cryptocurrency investments. Trend analysis serves as a cornerstone in the technical analyst's toolkit, offering a visual roadmap to navigate the ever-changing terrain of the crypto market.

6. Initial Coin Offerings (ICOs) and Token Sales

In the ever-evolving landscape of the cryptocurrency ecosystem, innovative fundraising methods have emerged as catalysts for groundbreaking projects and ventures. Among these, Initial Coin Offerings (ICOs) and token sales have captured the attention of entrepreneurs, investors, and enthusiasts alike. This introduction provides an overview of ICOs and token sales, delving into their origins, mechanisms, and significance within the broader blockchain industry.

The concept of Initial Coin Offerings can be traced back to 2013 when Mastercoin, a pioneering project built on the Bitcoin blockchain, conducted the first-ever ICO. Mastercoin's campaign marked a paradigm shift in fundraising methodologies, presenting a novel way for blockchain projects to secure capital. Inspired by this success, a wave of innovation ensued, with numerous projects adopting ICOs to fund development and engage with a global community of backers.

An Initial Coin Offering (ICO) is a fundraising method in which a project or startup issues digital tokens to the public in exchange for funding. These tokens, often built on blockchain platforms such as Ethereum, represent a form of ownership, utility, or future access to the project's services or products. Token sales, a broader term encompassing various fundraising mechanisms, include ICOs but may also refer to Security Token Offerings (STOs) and Initial Exchange Offerings (IEOs), each tailored to specific regulatory and project requirements.

ICO participants, called investors or contributors, typically acquire project-specific tokens using established cryptocurrencies like Bitcoin or Ethereum. The funds raised through the ICO are then allocated to project development, marketing, and other operational needs outlined in the project's whitepaper. This foundational document details the project's goals, technology, and the tokenomics governing the ICO.

Central to ICOs and token sales is tokenomics—the study of the economic models governing the issuance and use of tokens within a project's ecosystem. Tokenomics encompasses token distribution, utility, scarcity, and governance, shaping the economic dynamics and incentives for the project team and token holders.

While ICOs have facilitated the rapid growth of blockchain projects and decentralized platforms, they have not been without controversy. Concerns about regulatory compliance, fraudulent activities, and unsustainable fundraising practices have led regulatory bodies in various jurisdictions to develop frameworks for oversight. This has given rise to alternative fundraising methods like Security Token Offerings (STOs) that adhere to regulatory guidelines.

As the blockchain industry matures, ICOs and token sales continue to evolve. New fundraising models, such as Initial DEX Offerings (IDOs) and decentralized finance (DeFi) protocols, reflect the adaptability and creativity inherent in the blockchain space. These models aim to address challenges associated with traditional ICOs, providing increased transparency, liquidity, and compliance with regulatory standards.

Understanding the dynamics of ICOs and token sales in this ever-changing landscape is essential for investors and project teams. This exploration aims to provide insights into the foundations, mechanisms, and implications of ICOs and token sales, setting the stage for a deeper dive into the intricacies of this dynamic facet of the cryptocurrency realm.

Understanding ICOs and Token Sales

Initial Coin Offerings (ICOs) and token sales have become pivotal mechanisms for funding innovative projects in the decentralized blockchain technology. This chapter delves into a comprehensive understanding of ICOs and token sales, exploring their origins, mechanics, significance, and the evolving landscape of digital fundraising.

Explore the genesis of ICOs, tracing their roots back to the Mastercoin project in 2013. Discuss how this groundbreaking fundraising method has evolved, giving rise to various token sale models.

Differentiate between token sale models, including Security Token Offerings (STOs) and Initial Exchange Offerings (IEOs). Discuss how each model caters to specific project needs and regulatory considerations.

Explain the token creation process for ICOs, often utilizing blockchain platforms like Ethereum. Discuss the significance of intelligent contracts in automating the issuance and distribution of tokens.

Detail how participants in ICOs contribute funds, usually in established cryptocurrencies, and receive project-specific tokens in return. Explore token distribution mechanisms and the role of whitepapers in communicating project details.

Explore the utility of tokens within a project's ecosystem. Discuss how tokens may represent ownership, access to services, or governance rights, forming the basis of tokenomics—the economic model of a project.

Examine the role of scarcity in tokenomics and how it influences token value. Discuss the design of incentive structures to align the interests of project teams, investors, and users.

Discuss how ICOs have fueled rapid innovation and the development of decentralized platforms, enabling projects to engage a global community of backers.

Address the controversies surrounding ICOs, including concerns about regulatory compliance, fraud, and unsustainable fundraising practices. Explore how these challenges have prompted the development of alternative fundraising models.

Discuss how STOs have emerged as a regulated alternative to ICOs, incorporating legal compliance and asset-backed tokens.

Examine the concept of IEOs, where projects conduct token sales directly on cryptocurrency exchanges, leveraging the exchange's user base and reputation.

Explore the rise of Decentralized Finance (DeFi) platforms and Initial DEX Offerings (IDOs) as new paradigms in token sales, addressing liquidity and regulatory concerns.

Highlight the importance of transparent communication in whitepapers, ensuring clarity on project goals, technology, and tokenomics.

Discuss the significance of implementing robust security measures in ICOs to mitigate the risk of hacking and protect participant funds.

Discuss ongoing Innovations in the token sale space, such as integrating non-fungible tokens (NFTs) and exploring new fundraising models.

Explore the evolving regulatory frameworks for token sales globally and how they contribute to the legitimacy and sustainability of the fundraising model.

Understanding ICOs and token sales is paramount in navigating the dynamic landscape of blockchain fundraising. This chapter has provided a comprehensive overview, from the origins and mechanics to the evolving models and considerations for participants. As the industry continues to evolve, embracing new technologies and regulatory frameworks, the role of ICOs and token sales remains central to driving innovation and funding the decentralized projects that shape the future of blockchain technology.

Evaluating ICO Projects

Evaluating Initial Coin Offering (ICO) projects is a critical step for investors and enthusiasts looking to navigate the dynamic landscape of blockchain investments. This chapter provides a comprehensive guide on the key factors to consider when assessing the viability, potential, and risks of ICO projects.

Explore the foundational role of the whitepaper in communicating the project's vision, goals, technology, and tokenomics. Emphasize how a well-structured and transparent whitepaper is crucial for understanding the project's fundamentals.

Discuss strategies for critically analyzing the whitepaper, including assessing the clarity of project objectives, the feasibility of proposed solutions, and the transparency regarding token distribution and use.

Investigate the background, experience, and qualifications of the project's development team. Discuss the importance of a diverse and skilled team with expertise in blockchain development, project management, and relevant industries.

Examine the team's track record in successfully executing previous projects or contributions to the blockchain space. Evaluate the team's ability to navigate challenges and deliver on promises.

Analyze the token distribution plan outlined by the project. Discuss the importance of a well-balanced and fair distribution that aligns with the project's goals and incentives.

Evaluate the utility of the project's token within its ecosystem. Discuss how the token is used, its role in governance, and any mechanisms designed to incentivize holders and participants.

Assess the economic model for its sustainability. Explore how the project plans to generate and manage funds over the long term, considering factors such as inflation, deflation, and mechanisms for adapting to changing market conditions.

Examine the project's use of blockchain technology, consensus mechanisms, and overall technical infrastructure. Discuss how the project leverages technology to address specific challenges or provide innovative solutions.

Evaluate the project's competitive advantage in the market. Discuss any unique features, partnerships, or technological innovations that set the project apart from existing or potential competitors.

Assess the level of community engagement surrounding the project. Explore the community's size, activity, and sentiment on social media platforms, forums, and other channels.

Investigate the project's strategic partnerships with industry players, investors, or reputable organizations. Discuss how these partnerships contribute to the project's credibility, network, and potential for success.

Evaluate the project's regulatory compliance and adherence to legal frameworks. Discuss how regulatory uncertainties impact the project and how the team addresses potential regulatory challenges.

Assess the security measures implemented by the project to protect participant funds and sensitive information. Explore the project's resilience to potential cyber threats and vulnerabilities.

Discuss the importance of open and transparent communication channels between the project team and the community. Explore how responsive the team is to inquiries, concerns, and feedback.

Evaluate the frequency and quality of project updates. Discuss how timely and informative updates contribute to building trust and maintaining a positive relationship with the community.

Evaluating ICO projects requires a holistic approach, considering technical, economic, and community-related factors. By critically analyzing the whitepaper, team expertise, tokenomics, technology, community engagement, and risk factors, investors can make more informed decisions in the rapidly evolving landscape of blockchain investments. This comprehensive guide serves as a roadmap for navigating the complexities of ICO evaluations, empowering stakeholders to identify promising projects and contribute to the growth of the blockchain ecosystem.

Risks and Rewards of Participating in ICOs

Participating in Initial Coin Offerings (ICOs) presents a unique set of opportunities and challenges, with one prominent challenge being the need for more investor protection. This chapter explores the risks and rewards associated with the absence of regulatory safeguards and traditional investor protections in the ICO space.

Examine how the regulatory landscape for ICOs lacks uniformity globally, leading to varying levels of investor protection across jurisdictions. Discuss the challenges posed by this need for more consistency.

Discuss the absence of traditional legal safeguards, such as investor insurance and recourse mechanisms, available to participants in ICOs compared to conventional financial markets.

Explore the increased risk of fraudulent activities and scams without strict regulatory oversight, posing challenges for investors in distinguishing legitimate projects from malicious ones.

Discuss how the lack of investor protections may lead to reduced accountability among project teams, potentially resulting in mismanagement of funds or failure to deliver on promises.

Examine the susceptibility of the ICO market to manipulation, including pump-and-dump schemes, due to the absence of robust regulatory frameworks that monitor and deter such activities.

Discuss the potential rewards for investors who engage in ICOs, including early access to innovative blockchain projects that may not be available through traditional investment channels.

Explore the potential for high returns on investment in successful ICOs, where early participants may benefit from the appreciation of token values as the project gains traction and achieves milestones.

Emphasize the crucial role of due diligence in mitigating the risks associated with the lack of investor protections. Discuss how thorough research and analysis can help investors make informed decisions.

Guide investors on evaluating project transparency, thoroughly examining whitepapers, team backgrounds, and the overall clarity of the project's goals and operations.

Discuss how the industry has responded to the lack of investor protections by promoting best practices, transparency, and self-regulation within the blockchain and cryptocurrency community.

Explore initiatives to educate investors about the risks and rewards associated with ICO participation, empowering them to make informed decisions and navigate the landscape responsibly.

Provide insights into risk management strategies for investors participating in ICOs, including setting realistic expectations, diversifying portfolios, and staying vigilant against potential red flags.

Discuss ongoing regulatory developments and initiatives to enhance investor protections in the ICO space. Explore how evolving regulations may influence the dynamics of ICO participation.

Participating in ICOs offers a unique avenue for engaging with innovative blockchain projects, but the lack of investor protections introduces significant risks. By understanding these risks, conducting thorough due diligence, and staying informed about industry developments, investors can confidently navigate the ICO landscape. As the blockchain industry continues to mature, the balance between risks and rewards in ICO participation may evolve, influenced by regulatory advancements, industry initiatives, and the collective efforts of participants to foster a more secure and transparent ecosystem.

The initial Coin Offerings (ICO) landscape is dynamic, presenting participants with the promise of substantial rewards and, conversely, the inherent risks of project success and failure. This chapter delves into the intricacies of assessing and navigating the risks and rewards associated with the ultimate outcomes of ICO projects.

Define project success and failure within the context of ICOs. Explore the multifaceted nature of these outcomes, considering financial, technological, and community-related factors.

Discuss how success is not always binary and may manifest in different gradations, from meeting minimum project goals to achieving widespread adoption and market recognition.

Examine the risk of development setbacks leading to project failure. Discuss how technical challenges, delays, or the inability to deliver on the project's promises can impact its viability.

Discuss the risk of projects failing to gain traction in the market. Explore factors such as inadequate marketing, poor community engagement, or competition, which may contribute to a lack of adoption.

Explore the risk of mismanagement of funds by project teams, leading to financial insolvency. Discuss the importance of transparent financial reporting and sound financial practices.

Discuss how project success can result in the appreciation of token values, providing rewards for early investors. Explore scenarios where successful projects create demand for their native tokens.

Examine how successful projects contribute to the growth of their ecosystems. Discuss the positive impact of projects achieving their goals on the broader blockchain community.

Emphasize the critical role of due diligence in mitigating risks associated with project failure. Discuss the need for thorough research, analysis, and continuous monitoring.

Guide participants on evaluating project development roadmaps. Discuss how well-defined and realistic roadmaps indicate a team's commitment to project success.

Discuss strategies for mitigating risks through portfolio diversification. Explore how diversifying investments across multiple projects can help offset potential losses.

Encourage active participation in project communities. Discuss how staying engaged with project updates, developments, and community discussions can provide insights into the project's trajectory.

Explore case studies of both successful and failed ICOs. Discuss the lessons that can be gleaned from these experiences to inform future investment decisions.

Discuss how the blockchain community's understanding of success and failure in ICOs has evolved, leading to the development of more sophisticated evaluation criteria.

Project success and failure represent the dual nature of participating in ICOs, with potential rewards and risks interwoven. As participants navigate this dynamic landscape, understanding the factors contributing to success and failure is paramount. Through diligent research, active engagement, and a willingness to learn from successes and failures, participants can enhance their ability to make informed decisions and contribute to the maturation of the ICO ecosystem.

Participating in Initial Coin Offerings (ICOs) brings both potential rewards and inherent risks, with security risks and scams representing significant challenges. This chapter explores the multifaceted nature of security risks and scams associated with ICOs, providing insights into their various manifestations and strategies for safeguarding investments.

Define the landscape of security risks and scams, emphasizing the diversity of threats ranging from technical vulnerabilities to fraudulent schemes targeting unsuspecting investors.

Discuss the evolving nature of security risks and scams, highlighting how bad actors continually refine their tactics to exploit vulnerabilities in the ICO ecosystem.

Examine the prevalence of phishing attacks, where malicious entities attempt to deceive participants into revealing sensitive information such as private keys or login credentials.

Discuss the risks associated with smart contract vulnerabilities, including coding errors that may lead to exploits, loss of funds, or unauthorized access.

Explore the concept of token swap scams, where fraudulent projects encourage participants to exchange their tokens for a purportedly more valuable or exclusive token, resulting in financial losses.

Discuss malicious actors' creation of fake ICO projects, aiming to attract investments before disappearing with funds—a scenario commonly known as an exit scam.

Examine the risks associated with pump-and-dump schemes, where coordinated efforts artificially inflate the value of a token before orchestrating a rapid sell-off, leaving unsuspecting investors at a loss.

Highlight the importance of security audits conducted by reputable firms to identify and address vulnerabilities in intelligent contracts and project infrastructure.

Empower investors with strategies for conducting due diligence, including researching project teams, scrutinizing whitepapers, and verifying the authenticity of information.

Discuss the role of regulatory oversight in mitigating security risks and scams. Explore how adherence to legal frameworks can contribute to the legitimacy of ICO projects.

Examine the potential for legal safeguards to protect investors in the event of security breaches or fraudulent activities. Discuss the evolving legal landscape surrounding ICOs.

Encourage active involvement within the blockchain community to foster vigilance and the sharing of information regarding potential security risks and scams.

Discuss the importance of educational initiatives to raise awareness among participants, enabling them to recognize and avoid common security threats.

Navigating the landscape of security risks and scams in ICOs requires a proactive and informed approach. By staying vigilant, conducting thorough due diligence, and supporting regulatory efforts, participants can contribute to creating a more secure and trustworthy ICO ecosystem. The risks associated with security threats and scams underscore the importance of collective efforts to foster a resilient and reliable environment for blockchain innovation and investment.

Initial Coin Offerings (ICOs) have emerged as a groundbreaking fundraising mechanism, allowing startups and projects to access capital by issuing digital tokens. The allure of ICOs lies in their ability to democratize investment, providing opportunities for a global pool of investors to participate. However, the ICO landscape is riddled with regulatory uncertainties that overshadow the potential rewards. In this chapter, we explore the regulatory landscape surrounding ICOs and the associated risks and rewards for participants.

Before delving into regulatory uncertainties, it's crucial to understand the nature of ICOs. Essentially, ICOs involve the issuance of digital tokens, often built on blockchain technology, in exchange for cryptocurrency investments. These tokens may represent various assets, rights, or utilities within a project's ecosystem. ICOs gained popularity due to their ability to attract diverse investors, from retail enthusiasts to institutional players.

Lack of Regulations: ICOs operate in a regulatory gray area in many jurisdictions. The absence of clear regulations can leave investors without adequate legal recourse in cases of fraud, mismanagement, or project failure.

Fraudulent Activities: The decentralized and pseudonymous nature of blockchain makes it challenging to identify and prosecute fraudulent activities. Scams, Ponzi schemes, and pump-and-dump schemes have tarnished the ICO landscape.

Technological Risks: Many ICO projects are based on emerging technologies. Technical challenges, security vulnerabilities, or failure to deliver promised features pose inherent risks to investors.

Global Regulatory Fragmentation: The lack of a unified regulatory framework for ICOs has led to a fragmented global landscape. Each jurisdiction may have different definitions, classifications, and requirements, making it difficult for projects to navigate and comply with diverse regulations.

Securities Regulation: One of the primary regulatory challenges is determining whether tokens offered in an ICO qualify as securities. Securities regulations impose strict requirements, such as registration and disclosure, potentially hindering the flexibility and cost-effectiveness that ICOs promise.

Anti-Money Laundering (AML) and Know Your Customer (KYC): Regulatory uncertainties around AML and KYC requirements complicate ICOs. Striking a balance between user privacy and regulatory compliance is a persistent challenge.

Taxation: Tax treatment of ICOs varies widely across jurisdictions. Lack of clarity on tax implications can result in unexpected financial burdens for participants.

Access to Capital: ICOs provide a direct avenue for startups and projects to raise capital without the intermediaries of traditional fundraising methods, democratizing access to investment opportunities.

Global Reach: The borderless nature of blockchain technology allows ICOs to attract a global pool of investors, fostering a diverse and inclusive investor base.

Innovation and Disruption: ICOs have played a crucial role in funding innovative projects and disrupting traditional industries. This can lead to groundbreaking technological advancements and new business models.

Liquidity and Trading Opportunities: Tokens acquired through ICOs can offer liquidity and trading opportunities on various cryptocurrency exchanges, enabling investors to realize profits or adjust their portfolios.

Navigating the regulatory uncertainties surrounding ICOs requires a nuanced understanding of the legal landscape and a proactive approach to compliance. While the risks are significant, the rewards can be equally substantial for those who approach ICO participation with diligence and caution. As the regulatory environment evolves, staying informed and adapting to changes will be essential for both ICO projects and investors seeking to capitalize on this innovative fundraising mechanism.

One of the defining characteristics of the cryptocurrency landscape, and by extension, Initial Coin Offerings (ICOs), is the inherent market volatility. Cryptocurrency prices' dynamic and often unpredictable nature introduces a unique set of risks and rewards for participants. This chapter delves into the intricate relationship between market volatility, price fluctuations, and the potential impacts on ICO investors.

The cryptocurrency market operates 24/7, with global participation from many investors. Unlike traditional financial markets, crypto is still relatively young and lacks institutional maturity, contributing to stability. As a result, the market is susceptible to rapid and sometimes extreme price movements.

ICOs are often fueled by speculation, market sentiment, media coverage, and the promise of extraordinary returns. Positive news can trigger a surge in demand, while adverse developments can lead to sharp declines. The speculative nature of ICO investments amplifies market volatility.

Many tokens issued in ICOs may need more liquidity, meaning that large buy or sell orders can disproportionately impact the token's price. Thin order books can lead to slippage, where the execution price differs significantly from the expected price.

The value of tokens acquired through an ICO can experience rapid and substantial declines. Participants may hold assets worth significantly less than their initial investment, particularly without fundamental support for the token's value.

Margin trading, a common practice in cryptocurrency markets, can magnify losses during periods of high volatility. Participants using borrowed funds to invest in ICOs may face margin calls, leading to forced liquidation of their positions.

Sharp and sudden price movements can induce psychological stress among investors. Fear, uncertainty, and doubt (FUD) can lead to panic selling, exacerbating price fluctuations and contributing to a cycle of market instability.

Astute investors may leverage market volatility to capitalize on price discrepancies. Short-term traders can exploit price swings, executing well-timed trades to generate profits.

The early stages of an ICO often involve price discovery, allowing participants to acquire tokens at a potentially lower valuation. If the project gains traction, the subsequent increase in demand can drive up the token's value.

For investors with a diversified portfolio, market volatility in ICOs may have a mitigated impact. A well-structured portfolio that includes a mix of assets can help spread risk and reduce the overall impact of price fluctuations.

Comprehensive research into the fundamentals of the ICO project, including the team, technology, and roadmap, can provide a foundation for sound investment decisions. Understanding the underlying value proposition can help investors weather short-term price fluctuations.

Implementing risk management strategies, such as setting stop-loss orders and diversifying investments, can help protect against significant losses. Clear exit strategies and predetermined risk tolerances are crucial to effective risk management.

The cryptocurrency landscape is dynamic, with developments occurring rapidly. Staying informed about market trends, regulatory changes, and project updates is essential for making informed investment decisions and adapting to changing market conditions.

Market volatility and price fluctuations are integral aspects of the ICO ecosystem. While these dynamics pose risks, they also present opportunities for those approaching ICO participation with a well-informed and strategic mindset. By understanding the factors driving market volatility and implementing prudent risk management practices, participants can navigate the tumultuous waters of ICO investments and position themselves to capture potential rewards in this ever-evolving landscape.

7. Day Trading in Cryptocurrency

Day trading in the cryptocurrency market has become a captivating venture for many, driven by the promise of rapid returns and the allure of 24/7 market access. This chapter explores the intricacies of day trading in cryptocurrency, from understanding the fundamentals to developing effective strategies and managing the inherent risks.

Day trading involves the execution of short-term trades within a single trading day. The goal is to capitalize on intraday price movements, profiting from the volatility inherent in the cryptocurrency market.

Cryptocurrency markets are characterized by high volatility, providing ample opportunities for day traders to enter and exit positions. Understanding market trends, liquidity, and critical support/resistance levels is essential for successful day trading.

Day trading offers the potential for quick profits, but it comes with heightened risk. Traders must carefully balance risk and reward, prioritizing capital preservation while maximizing gains.

Technical analysis plays a central role in day trading. Traders use charts, indicators, and patterns to identify potential entry and exit points. Standard tools include moving averages, relative strength index (RSI), and Bollinger Bands.

Day traders can adopt various styles, with scalping and swing trading being popular choices. Scalpers aim to make small, frequent profits on short-term price fluctuations, while swing traders seek to capture more significant price movements over a slightly longer time frame.

Effective risk management is paramount. Traders should set stop-loss orders to limit potential losses, define position sizes based on risk tolerance, and avoid risking a significant portion of their capital on a single trade.

Stay attuned to news and events that could impact the cryptocurrency market. Significant announcements, regulatory developments, and macroeconomic factors can significantly influence prices and create trading opportunities.

Liquidity is crucial for day traders, ensuring that buy and sell orders can be executed at desired prices. Focus on cryptocurrency pairs with sufficient trading volume to avoid slippage and ensure smoother order execution.

Day traders thrive on volatility, but striking a balance is essential. Excessively volatile pairs may pose higher risks, while low-volatility pairs may need more price movements for profitable day trading.

Day trading can be emotionally taxing. Traders must maintain discipline and control emotions such as fear and greed. It is critical to establish, adhere to, and stick to a clear trading plan, regardless of short-term market fluctuations.

The cryptocurrency market is dynamic, and successful day traders continually educate themselves. Stay abreast of market trends, refine strategies, and learn from successes and failures to evolve as a trader.

While volatility provides opportunities, it also heightens the risk of substantial losses. Traders must be prepared for rapid and unpredictable price movements.

Day trading platforms often offer leverage, amplifying both gains and losses. Traders should exercise caution when using leverage and fully understand the associated risks.

Technical glitches, connectivity issues, and platform downtime can disrupt day trading activities. Implement backup plans and ensure reliable technology to mitigate these risks.

Day trading in cryptocurrency is a dynamic and potentially lucrative pursuit, but it requires a disciplined approach, continuous learning, and a keen understanding of market dynamics. By mastering the fundamentals, developing effective strategies, and navigating the psychological challenges, day traders can aim to capitalize on the opportunities presented by the ever-evolving cryptocurrency landscape.

Setting up a day trading plan is the cornerstone of success for any aspiring day trader in the cryptocurrency market. This chapter explores the essential elements of a comprehensive day trading plan, from defining goals to risk management and execution strategies.

Begin by establishing clear and realistic goals. Whether achieving a daily profit target, mastering a specific trading strategy, or building a consistent income stream, defining your objectives provides a roadmap for your day trading journey.

Assess your risk tolerance carefully. Understand the amount of capital you are willing to risk on a single trade and set overall risk limits for your daily activities. This step is crucial for preserving capital and managing emotions during turbulent market conditions.

Select cryptocurrency pairs based on liquidity, volatility, and your familiarity with the assets. Focus on a manageable number of pairs to avoid spreading yourself too thin and ensure in-depth knowledge of each.

Determine the time frames that align with your trading style. Day traders often work with short-term charts, such as 5-minute or 15-minute intervals, to capture intraday price movements.

Identify the technical analysis tools and indicators that align with your trading strategy. Standard tools include moving averages, relative strength index (RSI), and stochastic oscillators. Experiment with different combinations to find what works best for you.

Define your trading strategies based on technical analysis, such as trend following, breakout trading, or mean reversion. Clearly outline entry and exit criteria for each strategy, ensuring consistency in your decision-making process.

Determine the size of each position based on your risk tolerance and the percentage of your trading capital you're willing to risk on a single trade. Avoid overleveraging, as it can amplify both gains and losses.

Set stop-loss orders to limit potential losses on each trade. This automatic risk management tool helps enforce discipline and prevents emotional decision-making during market fluctuations.

Establish a minimum acceptable risk-reward ratio for your trades. For example, if your stop-loss represents a 1% loss, ensure that your profit target is at least 2%, providing a favorable risk-reward balance.

Conduct thorough pre-market analysis to identify potential trading opportunities, review market news, and assess overnight developments that could impact your chosen cryptocurrency pairs.

Clearly define your entry and exit points, including profit targets and stop-loss levels. Execute trades with discipline, avoiding impulsive decisions based on short-term market fluctuations.

Establish a daily trading routine with specific times for market analysis, trade execution, and performance review. Consistency fosters discipline and helps you adapt to changing market conditions.

Continuous Learning and Adaptation

Maintain a trading journal to record each trade, including the rationale behind your decisions, entry and exit points, and outcomes. Regularly review your journal to identify patterns, strengths, and areas for improvement.

Stay informed about market trends, new trading strategies, and technological developments. Attend webinars, read relevant literature, and engage with the trading community to foster continuous learning.

Crafting a robust day trading plan is fundamental to success in the cryptocurrency market. By defining clear goals, implementing effective risk management strategies, and maintaining a disciplined approach, day traders can navigate the complexities of the market and work towards achieving their objectives. Continuous learning, adaptation, and a commitment to self-improvement will contribute to long-term success in the dynamic world of day trading.

Day trading in cryptocurrencies can be both exhilarating and challenging. The volatile nature of the cryptocurrency market provides ample opportunities for profits but also comes with significant risks. Successful day traders understand the importance of implementing robust risk management strategies to safeguard their capital and navigate the turbulent waters of crypto trading.

Cryptocurrencies are renowned for their price volatility. Prices can experience rapid and unpredictable fluctuations within short time frames. Day traders must acknowledge and embrace this volatility while being prepared to manage the associated risks. Intraday price swings can be substantial, making risk management a critical aspect of day trading in the crypto space.

Establishing clear and realistic trading goals is fundamental to effective risk management. Day traders should define their profit targets and risk tolerance levels before entering a trade. Setting profit and loss limits helps maintain discipline and prevents emotional decision-making during trading sessions. By adhering to predetermined goals and limits, day traders can avoid impulsive actions driven by fear or greed.

Determining the appropriate position size is a crucial element of risk management. Day traders should calculate the size of their positions based on the percentage of their total trading capital they are willing to risk on a single trade. Additionally, using leverage can amplify both gains and losses in the crypto market. Traders should exercise caution and avoid excessive leverage, which can quickly erode capital during adverse market conditions.

Diversification is a key risk management strategy that spreads investments across different assets to reduce overall risk exposure. Day traders in cryptocurrency can diversify by trading various cryptocurrencies or incorporating traditional assets into their portfolios. Asset allocation helps balance risk and reward, enhancing the resilience of the trading strategy against market fluctuations.

Stop-loss orders are essential tools for managing risk in day trading. These orders automatically trigger a market exit when a specified price level is reached, limiting potential losses. Day traders should set stop-loss orders at strategic levels, considering both technical analysis and their risk tolerance. Regularly reviewing and adjusting stop-loss orders based on market conditions is critical to adapting to changing circumstances.

The cryptocurrency market evolves rapidly, and successful day traders must stay informed and adapt to new developments. Learning about market trends, technological advancements, and regulatory changes is crucial for effective risk management. By staying ahead of the curve, day traders can anticipate potential risks and adjust their strategies accordingly.

Day trading cryptocurrencies offers the potential for significant returns, but it comes with inherent risks. A well-defined risk management strategy is the cornerstone of a successful day trading career in the volatile crypto market. Traders who prioritize risk management, set realistic goals, diversify their portfolios, and employ practical tools such as stop-loss orders are better equipped to navigate the challenges and capitalize on the opportunities presented by day trading in cryptocurrencies.

Tools and Platforms for Crypto Day Trading

Day trading in cryptocurrencies can be both exhilarating and challenging. The volatile nature of the cryptocurrency market provides ample opportunities for profits but also comes with significant risks. Successful day traders understand the importance of implementing robust risk management strategies to safeguard their capital and navigate the turbulent waters of crypto trading.

Cryptocurrencies are renowned for their price volatility. Prices can experience rapid and unpredictable fluctuations within short time frames. Day traders must acknowledge and embrace this volatility while being prepared to manage the associated risks. Intraday price swings can be substantial, making risk management a critical aspect of day trading in the crypto space.

Establishing clear and realistic trading goals is fundamental to effective risk management. Day traders should define their profit targets and risk tolerance levels before entering a trade. Setting profit and loss limits helps maintain discipline and prevents emotional decision-making during trading sessions. By adhering to predetermined goals and limits, day traders can avoid impulsive actions driven by fear or greed.

Determining the appropriate position size is a crucial element of risk management. Day traders should calculate the size of their positions based on the percentage of their total trading capital they are willing to risk on a single trade. Additionally, using leverage can amplify both gains and losses in the crypto market. Traders should exercise caution and avoid excessive leverage, which can quickly erode capital during adverse market conditions.

Diversification is a key risk management strategy that spreads investments across different assets to reduce overall risk exposure. Day traders in cryptocurrency can diversify by trading various cryptocurrencies or incorporating traditional assets into their portfolios. Asset allocation helps balance risk and reward, enhancing the resilience of the trading strategy against market fluctuations.

Stop-loss orders are essential tools for managing risk in day trading. These orders automatically trigger a market exit when a specified price level is reached, limiting potential losses. Day traders should set stop-loss orders at strategic levels, considering both technical analysis and their risk tolerance. Regularly reviewing and adjusting stop-loss orders based on market conditions is critical to adapting to changing circumstances.

The cryptocurrency market evolves rapidly, and successful day traders must stay informed and adapt to new developments. Learning about market trends, technological advancements, and regulatory changes is crucial for effective risk management. By staying ahead of the curve, day traders can anticipate potential risks and adjust their strategies accordingly.

Day trading cryptocurrencies offers the potential for significant returns, but it comes with inherent risks. A well-defined risk management strategy is the cornerstone of a successful day trading career in the volatile crypto market. Traders who prioritize risk management, set realistic goals, diversify their portfolios, and employ practical tools such as stop-loss orders are better equipped to navigate the challenges and capitalize on the opportunities presented by day trading in cryptocurrencies.

8. Crypto Trading Strategies

Crypto trading, characterized by its 24/7 market, decentralized structure, and technological innovation, provides a unique landscape for traders seeking profit opportunities. However, the inherent risks and complexities of the crypto market necessitate a strategic approach. This introductory chapter delves into the fundamentals of crypto trading strategies, highlighting the importance of well-defined methodologies and adaptive techniques for navigating the ever-evolving crypto space.

The inception of Bitcoin in 2009 marked the genesis of a new era in finance. As the first decentralized cryptocurrency, Bitcoin paved the way for an expanding ecosystem of digital assets. Over the years, the crypto market has witnessed exponential growth, with thousands of cryptocurrencies and tokens now traded on various platforms. The market's maturation has given rise to diverse trading strategies, each tailored to exploit specific market conditions and trends.

Cryptocurrencies are renowned for their price volatility, distinguishing the crypto market from traditional financial markets. While volatility poses risks, it also presents lucrative opportunities for traders. Understanding and harnessing this volatility is fundamental to crafting effective trading strategies. From day trading to swing trading and long-term investing, strategies must be calibrated to navigate the market's inherent fluctuations.

Successful crypto trading hinges on a blend of fundamental and technical analysis. Fundamental analysis involves assessing the underlying factors that influence the value of a cryptocurrency, such as technology, adoption, and regulatory developments. Technical analysis, on the other hand, relies on historical price data and chart patterns to forecast future price movements. A well-rounded trading strategy often incorporates elements of both analyses to make informed decisions.

Amidst the allure of potential profits, risk management stands as the bedrock of every successful trading strategy. The unpredictable nature of the crypto market underscores the importance of protecting capital from substantial losses. Traders must implement risk management techniques, including setting stop-loss orders, diversifying portfolios, and sizing positions appropriately to safeguard against adverse market movements.

Crypto trading accommodates a spectrum of styles, each catering to individual traders' preferences and risk tolerance. Scalping involves making numerous small trades to capitalize on minimal price fluctuations, while day trading entails opening and closing positions within a single trading day. Swing trading extends the holding period to take advantage of medium-term trends, and long-term investing involves holding assets for extended periods based on a belief in their long-term potential.

The crypto market is constantly evolving, influenced by technological advancements, regulatory changes, and market sentiment. Successful traders must exhibit adaptability, staying attuned to emerging trends and adjusting their strategies accordingly. Embracing innovation, whether decentralized finance (DeFi) or non-fungible tokens (NFTs), can open new avenues for profitable trading.

As we explore crypto trading strategies, it is crucial to recognize that success in the crypto market is an ongoing journey of learning and adaptation. Each chapter that follows will delve into specific trading methodologies, techniques, and case studies, providing a comprehensive guide for traders seeking to navigate the multifaceted world of cryptocurrency trading. Whether you are a novice or an experienced trader, this guide aims to equip you with the knowledge and tools needed to navigate the complexities of crypto trading and thrive in this dynamic and innovative financial landscape.

Swing Trading Techniques

Swing is a style that captures shorter to medium-term price movements within an established trend. Unlike day trading, swing trading allows for a more relaxed approach, with positions typically held for several days to weeks. In the volatile world of cryptocurrencies, mastering swing trading techniques can enable traders to capitalize on both upward and downward price swings. This chapter explores various swing trading strategies, tools, and tips to help navigate the dynamic crypto market.

Swing trading relies heavily on the identification of trends. Traders must be adept at recognizing potential trend reversals or continuations. Technical analysis tools such as trendlines, moving averages, and the Relative Strength Index (RSI) can assist in pinpointing fundamental trend shifts. Understanding the prevailing market sentiment through social media, news, and on-chain analysis can also provide valuable insights into potential trend changes.

Support and resistance levels are crucial elements in swing trading. Support represents a price level at which a cryptocurrency tends to stop falling and may even bounce back, while resistance is a level where it often faces selling pressure. Identifying these levels through chart analysis enables traders to decide on entry and exit points. Utilizing tools like Fibonacci retracement levels can enhance the accuracy of identifying potential reversal zones.

Candlestick patterns visually represent price movements and can signal potential trend reversals or continuations. Patterns such as bullish engulfing, bearish engulfing, and doji can provide insights into market sentiment. With price action analysis, which examines the relationship between price movements and volume, traders can better understand market dynamics.

Moving averages are essential tools in swing trading. The crossover of short-term and long-term moving averages can signal the beginning of a new trend. The MACD indicator, which combines moving averages with additional features, provides further insights into the strength and direction of a trend. Swing traders often use these indicators to confirm trend changes and filter out false signals.

Maintaining a favorable risk-reward ratio is paramount in swing trading. Before entering a trade, traders should assess potential profit targets and set stop-loss orders to limit losses. Position sizing, determined by the percentage of total capital at risk, ensures that trades are appropriately scaled based on risk tolerance. This disciplined approach helps swing traders preserve capital and optimize returns over the long term.

While swing trading involves technical analysis, it's crucial to consider external factors such as news and events that may influence price movements. Unexpected developments, regulatory announcements, or significant partnerships can impact the crypto market. Staying informed about such events through news sources and social media can help swing traders anticipate and react to sudden market shifts.

Successful swing trading requires a well-defined trading plan. This plan should include straightforward entry and exit criteria, risk management strategies, and guidelines for adapting to changing market conditions. Traders should also test their strategy using historical data or paper trading before risking natural capital. Regularly reviewing and refining the trading plan ensures it remains relevant and effective in evolving market conditions.

Real-world examples and case studies offer valuable insights into applying swing trading techniques. Analyzing successful and unsuccessful trades, understanding the rationale behind decisions, and learning from wins and losses contribute to a trader's growth. Traders should maintain a journal to document their trades, strategies, and emotions, facilitating continuous improvement.

Swing trading demands flexibility and adaptability. Markets can change rapidly, and successful swing traders adjust their strategies accordingly. Being open to refining techniques, incorporating new indicators, and adapting to emerging trends ensures that swing traders remain resilient in the ever-evolving crypto landscape.

Swing trading in cryptocurrencies provides a balanced approach for traders seeking to capitalize on medium-term price movements. By combining technical analysis tools, risk management strategies, and a disciplined approach, swing traders can confidently navigate the crypto market. The following chapters will delve deeper into specific aspects of swing trading, offering a comprehensive guide to mastering this dynamic and versatile trading style.

Arbitrage Opportunities in the Crypto Market

Arbitrage, the practice of exploiting price differences of the same asset across different markets or platforms, has long been a strategy traders employ to capitalize on inefficiencies. In the cryptocurrency market, where prices can vary significantly between exchanges due to the decentralized and fragmented nature of the ecosystem, arbitrage opportunities abound. This chapter explores the fundamentals of crypto arbitrage, various types of arbitrage strategies, and the challenges and considerations associated with this dynamic trading approach.

Crypto arbitrage involves taking advantage of price differentials for the same cryptocurrency on different exchanges or markets. These discrepancies can arise due to factors such as varying levels of liquidity, geographical location, regulatory environments, or delays in information dissemination. The goal of arbitrage is to buy low on one platform and sell high on another, profiting from the price differential.

Spot arbitrage involves buying and selling the actual cryptocurrency on different exchanges. Traders exploit real-time price differences, executing trades promptly to capitalize on market inefficiencies.

Temporal arbitrage, or time-based arbitrage, capitalizes on price variations over time. Traders take advantage of price differences due to delays in information dissemination between exchanges, executing trades to profit from the delayed reaction of prices.

Cross-border arbitrage exploits price differences between the same cryptocurrency on exchanges in different geographic regions. Variations can arise due to regulatory differences, time zone disparities, or fluctuations in demand and supply.

Futures arbitrage involves capitalizing on price differences between the spot market and futures contracts. Traders can buy the underlying asset in the spot market and sell a futures contract, or vice versa, to profit from the price convergence over time.

Identifying arbitrage opportunities in the crypto market requires a combination of advanced tools and a keen understanding of market dynamics. Traders commonly use automated trading bots and algorithms that continuously monitor real-time price differentials across multiple exchanges. Additionally, market scanners, API integrations, and data analytics tools help streamline the identification and execution of arbitrage opportunities.

While arbitrage opportunities seem like risk-free trades, there are risks associated with execution delays, transaction costs, and sudden market fluctuations. Traders must implement effective risk management strategies, including setting stop-loss orders and ensuring potential profit justifies the associated costs and risks. Constant monitoring and quick execution are critical to mitigating risks in the fast-paced world of crypto arbitrage.

Crypto arbitrage has challenges. Markets can move swiftly, and delays in execution can erode potential profits. Additionally, transaction costs, withdrawal fees, and slippage must be carefully considered, as they can impact the overall profitability of arbitrage trades. Regulatory considerations and exchange policies also play a role, as some platforms may have restrictions or verification requirements that affect the efficiency of arbitrage strategies.

Successful crypto arbitrage often relies on leveraging technology and automation. Trading bots can execute trades swiftly and efficiently, ensuring that price differentials are exploited before they diminish. However, it's crucial to choose reliable and secure trading bot platforms and to monitor their performance continuously to adapt to changing market conditions.

Traders engaging in crypto arbitrage must know the tax implications of their activities. Profits from arbitrage are generally considered taxable income, and traders should maintain accurate records of their transactions for tax reporting purposes. Consultation with tax professionals is advisable to ensure compliance with local regulations.

Crypto arbitrage offers an intriguing avenue for traders to profit from market inefficiencies. By understanding the various types of arbitrage, employing advanced tools, managing risks effectively, and staying abreast of market dynamics, traders can navigate the challenges of this strategy. The following chapters will delve into specific arbitrage techniques, providing practical insights and guidance for those looking to explore and capitalize on arbitrage opportunities in the dynamic and evolving crypto market.

Combining Strategies for Optimal Results

In the multifaceted world of cryptocurrency trading, successful traders often find that employing a single strategy may only sometimes be sufficient to navigate the complexities of the market. Combining different trading strategies can provide a more comprehensive and adaptive approach, enhancing the potential for optimal results. This chapter explores the rationale behind combining strategies, provides insights into popular combination approaches, and discusses the considerations and benefits of this integrated approach to crypto trading.

Combining trading strategies allows traders to leverage the strengths of each approach while mitigating the weaknesses. Different strategies excel in various market conditions, and by employing a diversified approach, traders increase their adaptability to the ever-changing dynamics of the crypto market. Whether leveraging the speed of day trading, the precision of technical analysis, or the patience of long-term investing, a combined strategy approach seeks to optimize results across diverse market scenarios.

Combining swing trading and trend-following strategies can be effective. Swing trading captures short to medium-term price movements, while trend following ensures that traders participate in extended upward trends. This combination benefits traders from short-term volatility and the overarching market direction.

Integrating arbitrage with long-term investing provides a balanced approach. Arbitrage strategies capitalize on short-term price differentials, while long-term investing allows traders to hold assets for extended periods based on fundamental analysis. This combination balances opportunistic gains with a more patient investment horizon.

With its focus on short-term price movements, day trading can be complemented by fundamental analysis. While day trading relies on technical indicators and chart patterns, integrating fundamental analysis allows traders to make informed decisions based on a cryptocurrency's underlying value and potential.

Scalping, which involves making numerous small trades to capture minimal price fluctuations, can be enhanced through automation. Combining scalping with algorithmic or automated trading allows for quick execution and precise adherence to predefined criteria, optimizing the efficiency of the strategy.

Combining strategies inherently brings diversification to a trader's approach. Diversifying across different timeframes, methodologies, and market conditions helps mitigate risks associated with a single strategy and enhances overall portfolio resilience.

The crypto market is dynamic, and its conditions can change rapidly. Combining strategies enhances a trader's adaptability to various market scenarios. When one strategy may underperform in specific conditions, another may excel, allowing for a more resilient overall trading approach.

Effective risk management remains crucial in combined strategies. Traders must carefully consider the risk-reward ratios of each strategy and ensure that the overall risk exposure aligns with their risk tolerance. Balancing high-risk, high-reward strategy with more conservative approaches is critical.

Combining strategies requires a commitment to continuous learning and monitoring. Traders must stay informed about the performance of each strategy, adapt to changing market conditions, and be willing to refine or adjust their combined approach based on evolving circumstances.

Real-world examples and case studies offer valuable insights into the implementation and success of combined strategies. Analyzing how traders effectively navigate diverse market conditions provides practical guidance for optimizing their results through strategy combination.

Combining strategies in cryptocurrency trading is a dynamic and adaptive approach that capitalizes on the strengths of different methodologies. Traders seeking optimal results recognize the value of diversification, adaptability, and risk management in navigating the complexities of the crypto market. As we delve deeper into specific combined strategies in the following chapters, we aim to provide practical insights and guidance for traders who fine-tune their approach and achieve optimal results in their crypto trading endeavors.

9. Navigating Regulatory Challenges

The cryptocurrency landscape, characterized by innovation, decentralization, and rapid growth, has become a significant force in the global financial ecosystem. However, this disruptive nature also brings forth a myriad of regulatory challenges. As governments and regulatory bodies worldwide grapple with the emergence of cryptocurrencies, traders and investors face a dynamic and evolving regulatory environment. This chapter explores the key regulatory challenges in the crypto space, the impact of regulations on trading activities, and strategies for navigating this complex terrain.

Cryptocurrencies, born out of a desire for financial independence and decentralization, have encountered diverse regulatory responses from governments worldwide. The regulatory landscape is dynamic, with countries taking various approaches, from embracing cryptocurrencies to imposing strict regulations or outright bans. The lack of a universal regulatory framework challenges traders navigating the global crypto market.

Regulatory uncertainty remains one of the foremost challenges in the crypto space. Different jurisdictions interpret and regulate cryptocurrencies differently, creating a patchwork of rules and guidelines. Traders often need help understanding their obligations and the legal status of cryptocurrencies in various regions.

Governments are increasingly emphasizing compliance and AML measures in the crypto industry. Exchanges and trading platforms are subject to stringent Know Your Customer (KYC) requirements, requiring users to undergo identity verification. Navigating these compliance measures while preserving user privacy poses a delicate balance.

Taxation of cryptocurrency transactions varies widely across jurisdictions, and the need for standardized guidelines complicates matters for traders. Determining tax liabilities on capital gains, income from mining, and crypto-to-crypto transactions requires a nuanced understanding of local tax laws.

The emergence of security tokens, representing ownership in traditional assets, introduces additional layers of regulation. These tokens often fall under securities laws, requiring compliance with securities regulations, further complicating the legal landscape for traders and issuers.

Stringent regulations can impact market access and liquidity. Exchanges facing regulatory hurdles may limit their services, affecting specific cryptocurrencies' availability and trading volume. Traders must be mindful of the regulatory status of exchanges they use to ensure uninterrupted access.

Regulatory uncertainty can stifle innovation, particularly in Initial Coin Offerings (ICOs) and token offerings. Traders must be aware of the legal implications of participating in token sales, as regulatory crackdowns on unregistered securities can result in legal consequences.

Crypto traders often engage in cross-border transactions, raising jurisdictional challenges. Regulatory disparities between countries can impact the ease with which traders can conduct international transactions, necessitating a thorough understanding of cross-border regulatory frameworks.

Keeping abreast of regulatory developments is paramount. Traders should regularly monitor announcements from regulatory bodies, government agencies, and legal experts to stay informed about changes that may impact their activities.

Seeking advice from legal professionals specializing in cryptocurrency regulations can provide valuable insights. Legal guidance can help traders understand their obligations, assess compliance measures, and navigate the intricacies of local laws.

Diversification remains a fundamental strategy for managing regulatory risks. Traders should diversify their holdings across different cryptocurrencies and assets, reducing exposure to regulatory challenges specific to individual tokens or projects.

Opting for regulated exchanges enhances the likelihood of complying with local laws and regulations. Traders should prioritize platforms that adhere to KYC and AML requirements, reducing the risk of regulatory scrutiny.

Active participation in industry discussions and regulatory clarity advocacy can benefit the crypto community. Traders can contribute to the discourse on responsible regulations that foster innovation while ensuring consumer protection and market integrity.

Navigating regulatory challenges in cryptocurrency is a critical aspect of responsible trading. As governments worldwide grapple with the implications of digital assets, traders must adapt to the evolving regulatory landscape. By staying informed, engaging with legal professionals, diversifying portfolios, using regulated exchanges, and advocating for transparent and fair regulations, traders can navigate the complexities of the regulatory environment and contribute to the maturation of the crypto industry. In the subsequent chapters, we will delve deeper into specific regulatory considerations and provide practical insights for traders operating in this dynamic and evolving space.

Global Regulatory Landscape for Cryptocurrencies

The cryptocurrency revolution has transformed the financial landscape, introducing decentralized digital assets outside traditional banking systems. As this transformative technology gains widespread adoption, governments and regulatory bodies worldwide are grappling with the need to establish frameworks that balance innovation with consumer protection and market integrity. This chapter introduces the complex and dynamic global regulatory landscape for cryptocurrencies, exploring the diverse approaches taken by different jurisdictions, the key regulatory challenges faced by the industry, and the evolving nature of crypto regulations.

The rise of cryptocurrencies, led by the creation of Bitcoin in 2009, caught regulators off guard. Initially regarded with skepticism, cryptocurrencies have since grown into a substantial and influential market. Governments, recognizing the need for oversight, have begun crafting regulatory frameworks to address the unique challenges digital assets pose.

One of the defining features of the global regulatory landscape for cryptocurrencies is its diversity. Countries have taken varied approaches, from embracing and fostering innovation to imposing stringent regulations or outright bans. Some nations, like Switzerland and Singapore, have positioned themselves as crypto-friendly hubs, promoting the growth of blockchain technology and digital currencies. In contrast, others, like China and India, have imposed restrictions or outright bans, reflecting concerns over financial stability and investor protection.

The regulatory challenges faced by the cryptocurrency industry are multifaceted and continually evolving:

The absence of a standardized regulatory framework has led to uncertainty. Cryptocurrencies, classified differently in various jurisdictions, lack more uniformity, which hampers global consistency and compliance.

Global regulatory bodies are increasingly focusing on AML and KYC compliance in cryptocurrency. Striking a balance between these measures and user privacy has become a complex challenge for exchanges and traders.

Taxation of cryptocurrency transactions varies significantly from country to country. Determining tax liabilities for capital gains, mining income, and transactions involving different types of tokens adds a layer of complexity.

The emergence of security tokens has brought securities regulations into the crypto space, requiring compliance with intricate legal frameworks that impact issuance, trading, and ownership.

For participants in the crypto market, navigating the regulatory maze is akin to a delicate balancing act. Traders, investors, and industry stakeholders must adapt to the evolving nature of regulations while advocating for frameworks that foster innovation without compromising security or stability.

The global regulatory landscape directly influences market dynamics, affecting access, liquidity, and innovation. Regulatory developments can impact investor confidence and shape the trajectory of new projects and technologies within the crypto space.

As the crypto industry matures, there is a growing call for greater regulatory clarity and consistency. Stakeholders, including regulators, industry participants, and the broader community, are exploring avenues to establish more precise guidelines that balance fostering innovation and safeguarding the interests of users and investors.

The global regulatory landscape for cryptocurrencies is constantly changing, shaped by technological innovation, economic considerations, and the imperative for regulatory oversight. In subsequent chapters, we will explore specific regulatory considerations, challenges, and strategies for traders and industry participants navigating this intricate and evolving terrain. Understanding the nuances of global regulations is paramount for those seeking to engage responsibly and effectively in the dynamic world of cryptocurrency.

(a) Cross-Border Trading Challenges: Harmonizing Regulations for International Transactions

In the decentralized and globalized world of cryptocurrencies, the notion of borders fades as digital assets traverse the globe within seconds. While this cross-border accessibility presents opportunities for traders, it also introduces many challenges stemming from the lack of uniform regulatory frameworks across jurisdictions. This chapter explores the complexities of cross-border trading in cryptocurrency, the challenges traders face, and the imperative need for harmonizing regulations to facilitate seamless and secure international transactions.

The borderless nature of cryptocurrencies has been a central tenet of their appeal, promising frictionless and efficient international transactions. Traders can access a global marketplace, but this advantage comes with challenges, including regulatory disparities, legal uncertainties, and varying compliance requirements.

Cryptocurrencies encounter diverse regulatory landscapes as they traverse different jurisdictions. Countries have adopted varying stances, from embracing digital assets to implementing restrictive measures or outright bans. This regulatory patchwork introduces uncertainty for traders engaging in cross-border transactions as they navigate different legal frameworks, compliance obligations, and reporting standards.

The Know Your Customer (KYC) and Anti-Money Laundering (AML) requirements, crucial for regulatory compliance, can present significant challenges in cross-border trading. Traders and exchanges must contend with differing KYC standards, making maintaining a streamlined and efficient onboarding process for users across various regions challenging.

Tax implications further complicate cross-border trading. Cryptocurrency transactions may be subject to varying tax treatments in different jurisdictions, impacting the overall profitability of trades. Understanding and complying with these diverse tax regulations is essential for traders to avoid legal complications and financial penalties.

The decentralized nature of cryptocurrencies raises jurisdictional challenges. In the absence of a globally recognized legal framework, disputes arising from cross-border transactions can lead to legal uncertainties. Traders may be subject to conflicting legal interpretations and face challenges in seeking legal redress.

Harmonizing regulations on an international scale is a critical step toward addressing the challenges of cross-border trading. A coordinated effort among nations to establish common standards, regulations, and reporting requirements can create a more conducive environment for international transactions. Such harmonization could encompass:

We are establishing uniform definitions for cryptocurrencies and related terms to provide clarity and consistency in legal interpretation across borders.

We are formulating international tax agreements to address the taxation challenges associated with cross-border cryptocurrency transactions and provide a framework for equitable and transparent tax treatment.

International organizations and collaborations play a pivotal role in fostering regulatory harmonization. Forums such as the Financial Action Task Force (FATF) and the International Organization of Securities Commissions (IOSCO) provide platforms for regulatory bodies to collaborate, share best practices, and work toward establishing global standards.

Harmonizing regulations for cross-border trading offers several benefits for traders:

Streamlined and standardized regulatory requirements lessen the compliance burden on traders and exchanges, enabling more efficient cross-border transactions.

Clear and consistent regulations provide traders with legal certainty, reducing the risk of disputes and legal challenges arising from cross-border transactions.

Harmonization fosters a more open and interconnected global market, allowing traders more significant access to diverse assets and trading opportunities.

As the cryptocurrency landscape continues to evolve, the challenges and opportunities associated with cross-border trading remain central to the industry's growth. Achieving regulatory harmonization represents a collaborative effort involving governments, regulatory bodies, international organizations, and industry stakeholders. In the subsequent chapters, we will explore specific considerations for traders engaging in cross-border transactions and strategies to navigate the complexities of this globalized crypto landscape.

(b) <u>Regulatory Implications of Decentralized Finance (DeFi)
and Non-Fungible Tokens (NFTs)</u>

The rapid rise of Decentralized Finance (DeFi) and Non-Fungible Tokens (NFTs) has ushered in a new era of innovation in the cryptocurrency space. While these advancements bring novel user opportunities, they pose unique global regulatory challenges for governments and regulatory bodies. This chapter delves into the regulatory implications of DeFi and NFTs, exploring the evolving legal landscape, challenges faced by regulators, and considerations for participants in these decentralized ecosystems.

Decentralized Finance, or DeFi, represents a paradigm shift in traditional financial services by utilizing blockchain technology to create open and accessible economic systems. DeFi protocols facilitate lending, borrowing, trading, and other financial activities without conventional intermediaries. However, this decentralized nature introduces regulatory complexities.

Non-fungible tokens (NFTs) are unique cryptographic tokens representing ownership or proof of authenticity of digital or physical assets. NFTs have gained immense popularity for their application in digital art, collectibles, gaming, and virtual real estate. As unique assets on the blockchain, NFTs present regulatory challenges related to ownership, copyright, and securities regulations.

DeFi platforms operate without traditional financial intermediaries, raising questions about accountability, consumer protection, and the role of decentralized governance.

Using smart contracts in DeFi introduces challenges related to code vulnerabilities, security breaches, and the enforceability of contractual agreements without a centralized legal framework.

NFTs often represent digital content subject to copyright laws. Regulatory challenges arise concerning ownership, licensing, and the protection of intellectual property rights within decentralized ecosystems.

The NFT market is susceptible to fraudulent activities, including fake listings, plagiarism, and market manipulation, prompting regulatory concerns around consumer protection and market integrity.

NFTs with investment-like characteristics may fall under securities regulations. Determining the regulatory status of NFTs becomes complex when they represent fractionalized ownership or revenue-sharing agreements.

Regulators worldwide are adapting to the challenges posed by DeFi and NFTs, recognizing the need to strike a balance between fostering innovation and protecting consumers. Responses include:

Some regulatory bodies provide guidance and frameworks to assist DeFi projects and NFT platforms in navigating legal requirements and ensuring compliance.

Collaborative efforts between regulators and industry stakeholders aim to foster open dialogue, share best practices, and develop regulatory solutions that accommodate the unique characteristics of decentralized technologies.

DeFi and NFT ecosystem participants should conduct thorough legal, due diligence to understand the regulatory implications of their activities and the platforms they engage with.

Mitigating smart contract risks, understanding the legal status of NFTs, and implementing robust risk management practices are essential for participants in these decentralized ecosystems.

The regulatory landscape for DeFi and NFTs is evolving, shaped by ongoing dialogue, regulatory experiments, and collaborative efforts. As these technologies mature, regulatory frameworks will likely become more defined, providing more precise guidelines for industry participants and regulators.

Participating in the decentralized realms of DeFi and NFTs requires a nuanced understanding of the evolving regulatory landscape. As governments and regulatory bodies continue to adapt, participants must stay informed, engage in responsible practices, and contribute to the ongoing dialogue shaping the future of decentralized finance and non-fungible tokens. In the following chapters, we will explore specific considerations and strategies for navigating the regulatory implications of these groundbreaking technologies.

(c) <u>Regulatory Implications of Decentralized Finance (DeFi) and Non-Fungible Tokens (NFTs)</u>

The rapid rise of Decentralized Finance (DeFi) and Non-Fungible Tokens (NFTs) has ushered in a new era of innovation in the cryptocurrency space. While these advancements bring novel user opportunities, they pose unique global regulatory challenges for governments and regulatory bodies. This chapter delves into the regulatory implications of DeFi and NFTs, exploring the evolving legal landscape, challenges faced by regulators, and considerations for participants in these decentralized ecosystems.

Decentralized Finance, or DeFi, represents a paradigm shift in traditional financial services by utilizing blockchain technology to create open and accessible economic systems. DeFi protocols facilitate lending, borrowing, trading, and other financial activities without conventional intermediaries. However, this decentralized nature introduces regulatory complexities.

Non-fungible tokens (NFTs) are unique cryptographic tokens representing ownership or proof of authenticity of digital or physical assets. NFTs have gained immense popularity for their application in digital art, collectibles, gaming, and virtual real estate. As unique assets on the blockchain, NFTs present regulatory challenges related to ownership, copyright, and securities regulations.

DeFi platforms operate without traditional financial intermediaries, raising questions about accountability, consumer protection, and the role of decentralized governance.

Using smart contracts in DeFi introduces challenges related to code vulnerabilities, security breaches, and the enforceability of contractual agreements without a centralized legal framework.

NFTs often represent digital content subject to copyright laws. Regulatory challenges arise concerning ownership, licensing, and the protection of intellectual property rights within decentralized ecosystems.

The NFT market is susceptible to fraudulent activities, including fake listings, plagiarism, and market manipulation, prompting regulatory concerns around consumer protection and market integrity.

 NFTs with investment-like characteristics may fall under securities regulations. Determining the regulatory status of NFTs becomes complex when they represent fractionalized ownership or revenue-sharing agreements.

Regulators worldwide are adapting to the challenges posed by DeFi and NFTs, recognizing the need to strike a balance between fostering innovation and protecting consumers. Responses include:

Some regulatory bodies provide guidance and frameworks to assist DeFi projects and NFT platforms in navigating legal requirements and ensuring compliance.

Collaborative efforts between regulators and industry stakeholders aim to foster open dialogue, share best practices, and develop regulatory solutions that accommodate the unique characteristics of decentralized technologies.

DeFi and NFT ecosystem participants should conduct thorough legal, due diligence to understand the regulatory implications of their activities and the platforms they engage with.

Mitigating smart contract risks, understanding the legal status of NFTs, and implementing robust risk management practices are essential for participants in these decentralized ecosystems.

The regulatory landscape for DeFi and NFTs is evolving, shaped by ongoing dialogue, regulatory experiments, and collaborative efforts. As these technologies mature, regulatory frameworks will likely become more defined, providing more precise guidelines for industry participants and regulators.

Participating in the decentralized realms of DeFi and NFTs requires a nuanced understanding of the evolving regulatory landscape. As governments and regulatory bodies continue to adapt, participants must stay informed, engage in responsible practices, and contribute to the ongoing dialogue shaping the future of decentralized finance and non-fungible tokens. In the following chapters, we will explore specific considerations and strategies for navigating the regulatory implications of these groundbreaking technologies.

Legal Considerations in the Crypto Space

The decentralized and dynamic cryptocurrency space introduces many legal considerations that participants must navigate to operate responsibly and avoid legal pitfalls. This chapter explores vital legal aspects relevant to the crypto industry, covering regulatory compliance, contractual agreements, intellectual property concerns, tax implications, and potential legal challenges that may arise in this evolving landscape.

Participants in the crypto space must be aware of and comply with the regulatory requirements specific to their jurisdictions. Regulations vary widely, covering licensing, consumer protection, and Anti-Money Laundering (AML) measures.

Implementing robust Anti-Money Laundering (AML) and Know Your Customer (KYC) procedures is crucial. Ensuring compliance with these measures aligns with regulatory expectations and enhances the security and integrity of crypto transactions.

Projects involving security tokens must adhere to securities regulations. Determining whether a token qualifies as a security and navigating the associated regulatory requirements is essential for legal compliance.

Smart contracts must be carefully drafted and audited to avoid vulnerabilities and code-related legal issues while automating and enhancing transaction trust. Conducting thorough code audits is essential to identify and rectify potential risks.

Token sale agreements, such as Initial Coin Offerings (ICOs) or Token Generation Events (TGEs), should be well-drafted to outline the terms and conditions of the token sale clearly. Ensuring transparency and adherence to legal standards is vital to avoid regulatory scrutiny.

Agreements with collaborators, developers, and other stakeholders should be well-defined. Clearly outlining roles, responsibilities, and compensation structures helps prevent disputes and ensures legal clarity in collaborative ventures.

Projects must consider the intellectual property implications of their tokens and underlying protocols. Clear identification and protection of unique features, codebases, and innovations help safeguard intellectual property rights.

NFTs often represent digital art or media subject to copyright laws. Navigating copyright issues, licensing agreements, and establishing ownership rights are crucial considerations in the NFT space.

Traders and investors must understand the tax implications of their activities, including capital gains on cryptocurrency investments and income tax on mining rewards or trading profits.

Accepting cryptocurrency payments for goods and services may trigger Value-Added Tax (VAT) or Goods and Services Tax (GST) obligations. Businesses must be aware of and comply with tax requirements related to cryptocurrency transactions.

With a centralized legal framework, resolving disputes related to crypto transactions can be simple. Engaging in dispute resolution mechanisms, including arbitration or mediation, can be valuable for swift and effective conflict resolution.

The regulatory landscape is subject to rapid changes. Staying informed and maintaining agility in response to evolving regulations helps participants adapt to new legal requirements and avoid non-compliance issues.

Participants in the crypto space, especially exchanges and token issuers, should adhere to principles of transparency and fair practices. Clear communication with users and investors is essential to comply with consumer protection laws.

Navigating the legal landscape in the crypto space requires a comprehensive understanding of regulatory requirements, innovative contractual practices, intellectual property considerations, tax implications, and potential legal challenges. As the industry matures, participants must prioritize legal compliance and stay proactive in addressing emerging legal issues. The following chapters will delve into more specific legal considerations and offer practical insights to help navigate the cryptocurrency space's complex and evolving legal terrain.

10. Security and Risk Mitigation

Cryptocurrencies have emerged as a transformative force, promising decentralization, transparency, and financial inclusion. However, as the adoption of cryptocurrencies accelerates, so does the need for robust security measures and effective risk mitigation strategies. This chapter delves into the critical aspects of security and risk mitigation within cryptocurrency, exploring this dynamic field's challenges, opportunities, and evolving landscape.

The genesis of cryptocurrency, marked by the introduction of Bitcoin in 2009, brought about a paradigm shift in traditional finance. Blockchain technology, the underlying foundation of most cryptocurrencies, introduced a decentralized and tamper-resistant ledger, challenging the conventional financial system. As the popularity of cryptocurrencies surged, so did the risks associated with their use, including hacking, fraud, and regulatory uncertainties.

Security lies at the core of cryptocurrency adoption and sustained growth. The decentralized nature of blockchain networks does not make them immune to security threats. Cryptocurrency transactions, wallets, and exchanges are susceptible to risks such as hacking, phishing, and insider threats. The consequences of security breaches are financial and can erode trust in the entire cryptocurrency ecosystem.

Understanding the diverse risks and threat vectors in cryptocurrency is imperative for adequate security and risk mitigation. Threats may emanate from technological vulnerabilities, regulatory uncertainties, market manipulation, or social engineering attacks. This chapter will explore these risk factors in detail, providing insights into the multifaceted challenges faced by cryptocurrency stakeholders.

The regulatory environment for cryptocurrencies is evolving globally. Governments and regulatory bodies are grappling with balancing fostering innovation and protecting consumers. A comprehensive overview of the current regulatory landscape will be provided, shedding light on the compliance requirements and legal frameworks that shape the cryptocurrency industry.

In response to the growing risks, the cryptocurrency community has developed a range of security measures and best practices. This chapter will explore the tools and techniques available to safeguard cryptocurrency assets, from secure wallet management to multi-signature authentication and cold storage solutions. Additionally, it will discuss the importance of education and awareness in promoting safe practices among users.

Beyond preventive measures, risk mitigation strategies play a pivotal role in ensuring the resilience of cryptocurrency systems. This section will delve into risk assessment methodologies, contingency planning, and crisis management, offering a comprehensive guide to address and mitigate potential risks proactively.

As technology advances and the cryptocurrency landscape continues to evolve, the future of security will be shaped by innovative solutions and adaptive strategies. This chapter will conclude with a glimpse into emerging trends, technologies, and research initiatives that promise to enhance the security and risk mitigation landscape in the cryptocurrency domain.

As we navigate the complexities of this transformative technology, understanding and addressing the challenges of security and risk management become paramount for the sustained success and widespread adoption of cryptocurrencies.

Protecting Your Crypto Assets

As blockchain transactions' decentralized and pseudonymous nature provides both opportunities and challenges, this chapter aims to guide users through a comprehensive set of strategies and best practices to ensure the security of their crypto holdings.

Before delving into protective measures, it is crucial to comprehend the diverse threats that crypto holders may face. Threats range from external factors such as hacking, phishing, and malware attacks to internal risks like the mishandling of private keys or engaging in insecure transactions. An awareness of these threats forms the foundation for adequate protection.

The choice of wallet significantly influences the security of your crypto assets. This section will explore the two primary types of wallets—hardware and software—and discuss their advantages and vulnerabilities. Best practices for secure wallet management, including cold storage and multi-signature authentication, will be highlighted to mitigate the risk of unauthorized access.

The private key is the linchpin of crypto security. This chapter will underscore the importance of securely storing and managing secret keys. Topics covered include key generation, secure backup procedures, and strategies to prevent critical exposure. Users will gain insights into the role of hardware security modules (HSMs) and the importance of maintaining complete control over their private keys.

Executing secure transactions is fundamental to protecting crypto assets. This section will guide users through best practices when sending and receiving funds, emphasizing double-checking recipient addresses, utilizing QR codes, and employing secure connections. Innovative contract security considerations will also be addressed to prevent vulnerabilities in decentralized applications.

Maintaining a proactive approach to security involves regular audits and monitoring of your crypto holdings. Users will learn the importance of reviewing transaction histories, monitoring account access, and utilizing blockchain explorers. Additionally, this section will cover the significance of staying informed about potential security vulnerabilities in the chosen wallet or exchange.

Enhancing security through additional layers of authentication is crucial. The chapter will delve into the benefits of Two-Factor Authentication (2FA) and explore the emerging trend of biometric authentication for crypto assets. Users will learn how these methods add an extra layer of protection against unauthorized access.

Social engineering attacks and phishing attempts often target crypto holders. This section will provide practical guidance on recognizing and avoiding common social engineering tactics and phishing schemes. Education and awareness are vital components of defense against these types of attacks.

Preparing for the unexpected is a responsible aspect of crypto asset protection. This chapter will conclude by discussing estate planning for digital assets and inheritance solutions. Users will be guided in creating a secure and accessible plan for their crypto holdings in the event of unforeseen circumstances.

In summary, protecting your crypto assets requires a multifaceted approach encompassing secure storage, vigilant transaction practices, and a deep understanding of potential threats. By adopting the strategies and best practices outlined in this chapter, users can fortify their defenses and navigate the crypto landscape with confidence in the security of their digital assets.

Common Scams and How to Avoid Them

Cryptocurrencies' decentralized and pseudonymous nature creates a fertile ground for various scams and fraudulent activities. This chapter aims to equip users with the knowledge and awareness needed to identify and steer clear of common scams prevalent in the crypto space.

Phishing attacks remain a persistent threat in the crypto world. This section will explore the various forms of phishing, including email and website impersonation. Readers will learn to recognize red flags, verify website URLs, and implement secure communication practices to protect themselves from phishing attempts.

Ponzi schemes and HYIPs promise high returns with little risk, preying on the desire for quick profits. This part of the chapter will delve into the characteristics of these scams, helping users identify warning signs and avoid investment traps that promise unrealistic returns.

The Initial Coin Offering (ICO) model has been a scam breeding ground. This section will provide insights into how users can distinguish between legitimate ICOs and fraudulent token sales. Topics include scrutinizing whitepapers, researching project teams, and verifying partnerships.

Pump and dump schemes involve artificially inflating the price of a cryptocurrency to attract investors and then quickly selling off the inflated asset. This section will discuss the mechanics of pump-and-dump schemes, enabling users to recognize market manipulation and make informed investment decisions.

Social engineering attacks exploit human psychology to manipulate individuals into divulging sensitive information. This chapter will shed light on common social engineering tactics in crypto, emphasizing the importance of skepticism and secure communication practices.

Fraudulent wallets and exchanges pose a significant threat to crypto users. This section will guide readers on identifying and avoiding fake wallets and exchanges by conducting thorough research, checking for user reviews, and verifying the legitimacy of the service provider.

Social media platforms are often used to promote pump-and-dump schemes. Users will gain an understanding of how these schemes operate on platforms like Telegram and Twitter and learn how to identify and steer clear of groups that manipulate market prices for profit.

Impersonation scams involve fake social media profiles and communication channels that mimic legitimate entities. This section will guide you in verifying the authenticity of communication channels, recognizing impersonation attempts, and ensuring secure interactions.

Community awareness plays a pivotal role in combating scams in the interconnected world of cryptocurrencies. This chapter will conclude by highlighting the importance of sharing information, reporting scams, and contributing to the collective effort to create a safer crypto environment.

Understanding common scams and developing a skeptical mindset is essential for navigating the crypto space securely. By familiarizing themselves with the information presented in this chapter, users can fortify their defenses against the diverse range of scams prevalent in the cryptocurrency ecosystem.

Insurance and Custodial Services in Cryptocurrency

As the cryptocurrency ecosystem matures, the need for robust risk management and secure storage solutions has led to the development of insurance and custodial services. This chapter explores the evolving landscape of these services, shedding light on their significance, challenges, and contributions to the broader adoption of digital assets.

Cryptocurrencies, while offering unique advantages, come with inherent risks. The potential for financial loss is real, from exchange hacks to operational errors. This section examines the necessity of insurance in the crypto space, addressing the concerns of investors and institutions regarding the safety and security of their digital assets.

Cryptocurrency insurance has various forms, covering different aspects of the digital asset ecosystem. This chapter will categorize and explain the types of insurance available, including coverage for custodial services, cyber theft, regulatory changes, and errors and omissions.

Custodial services are critical in providing institutional and individual investors with secure storage solutions. This section explores the functions of custodial services, emphasizing the importance of institutional-grade security measures, cold storage, and comprehensive risk management protocols.

Despite the growing interest in crypto-insurance, there are challenges unique to this nascent industry. This section discusses the hurdles insurers face, including regulatory uncertainties, the lack of historical data, and the volatile nature of cryptocurrency markets. Understanding these challenges is crucial for both insurers and those seeking coverage.

The regulatory environment for crypto insurance and custodial services is continually evolving. This part of the chapter provides an overview of the current regulatory landscape, addressing the efforts made by authorities to establish guidelines and standards for these services. Regulatory compliance is integral to fostering trust in the sector.

For investors entrusting their assets to custodial services, careful consideration is paramount. This section offers a guide to selecting reputable custodians, covering factors such as security measures, insurance coverage, transparency, and track record. These best practices empower users to decide where to store their digital assets.

Institutional investors, with their stringent risk management requirements, play a pivotal role in the broader adoption of cryptocurrencies. This chapter explores how custodial services contribute to institutional adoption by providing the security and compliance necessary for large-scale investment.

As the cryptocurrency industry evolves, so do insurance and custodial services. This section provides a glimpse into emerging trends, such as decentralized finance (DeFi) insurance and the integration of artificial intelligence for risk assessment. Understanding these trends is essential for staying ahead in the rapidly changing landscape.

Integrating insurance and custodial services marks a significant step toward enhancing the cryptocurrency ecosystem's security and risk management practices. As these services mature, their role in fostering confidence among investors, institutions, and the broader public becomes increasingly vital for the sustained growth and adoption of digital assets.

11. Case Studies: Crypto Millionaires

A new class of wealth has emerged – the Crypto Millionaires. Born out of blockchain technology's innovative and decentralized nature, these individuals have navigated the volatile crypto markets to amass significant fortunes. This chapter introduces a series of case studies that delve into the stories, strategies, and experiences of these crypto millionaires, offering a glimpse into the diverse paths that have led individuals to financial success in the digital asset realm.

The advent of Bitcoin in 2009 marked the beginning of a financial revolution, introducing the concept of decentralized and borderless digital currencies. As the crypto landscape expanded beyond Bitcoin, with the creation of thousands of altcoins and the emergence of blockchain technology, opportunities for financial gains multiplied. This section explores the foundational elements of the crypto revolution that set the stage for the creation of crypto millionaires.

The meteoric rise in the value of cryptocurrencies, particularly during bull markets, has created a unique class of wealth. From early Bitcoin adopters to savvy traders and innovative blockchain entrepreneurs, this chapter will provide an overview of the diverse backgrounds and entry points propelling individuals into the coveted realm of crypto millionaires.

Crypto millionaires have achieved their status through various investment strategies, including long-term holding, active trading, and participation in initial coin offerings (ICOs) or token sales. This section will explore the different investment approaches adopted by crypto millionaires, shedding light on the risk-reward dynamics that have shaped their financial journeys.

The heart of this chapter lies in the exploration of individual case studies. These narratives will highlight the journeys of selected crypto millionaires, detailing their backgrounds, the key decisions that led to their success, and the challenges they encountered along the way. Through these case studies, readers will gain valuable insights into the multifaceted nature of crypto wealth accumulation.*

While the stories of crypto millionaires are often inspirational, they also carry important lessons. This section will extract critical takeaways from the case studies, offering insights into successful strategies, risk management practices, and common pitfalls that aspiring crypto investors should be mindful of in their journeys.

Beyond individual success stories, the emergence of crypto millionaires has broader socio-economic implications. This section will explore the influence of crypto wealth on industries, philanthropy, and the traditional financial landscape, as well as the challenges and controversies associated with this newfound form of prosperity.

As the crypto space continues to evolve, so will the opportunities and challenges for those seeking to join the ranks of crypto millionaires. This section will speculate on the future trends, potential disruptors, and emerging narratives that could shape the next generation of wealth creation in the digital asset space.

As we delve into these individuals' personal and financial journeys, the aim is to provide readers with valuable insights, inspiration, and a nuanced understanding of the factors that contribute to success in the dynamic world of cryptocurrency wealth creation.

Success Stories in Crypto Investments

Cryptocurrencies and success stories abound, showcasing the transformative potential of digital assets as vehicles for wealth creation. This chapter delves into a collection of compelling success stories, each illustrating individuals' unique paths to achieve financial prosperity through strategic and often pioneering crypto investments.

The chapter opens with an overview of how individuals have found success in the crypto investment landscape. From early Bitcoin adopters to those who navigated the complexities of ICOs and decentralized finance (DeFi), these success stories provide valuable insights into the strategies, decisions, and circumstances that led to financial triumph.

Some of the earliest crypto success stories involve individuals who recognized the revolutionary potential of Bitcoin in its infancy. This section explores the narratives of those who invested in Bitcoin in its nascent stages, witnessing exponential growth as the cryptocurrency gained widespread adoption and recognition.

The Initial Coin Offering (ICO) boom presented a unique opportunity for investors to participate in the launch of new blockchain projects. This section delves into the success stories of individuals who identified promising ICOs, invested early, and reaped substantial rewards as these projects matured and gained traction within the crypto space.

Success in crypto investments often involves a deep understanding of market dynamics and effective trading strategies. This part of the chapter explores the stories of traders who honed their skills in technical analysis, timing the market, and navigating volatility to accumulate significant wealth through astute trading practices.

The rise of decentralized finance (DeFi) has opened up new avenues for crypto success. This section delves into the narratives of individuals who explored the innovative world of decentralized lending, yield farming, and governance tokens, showcasing how they leveraged the opportunities presented by the DeFi ecosystem.

Throughout the success stories, common themes and strategies emerge. This section distills critical lessons from the featured individuals, emphasizing the importance of thorough research, risk management, and a diversified approach to crypto investments. Readers will gain actionable insights to inform their investment strategies.

Success in the crypto space has its challenges. This section explores the obstacles individuals face in their journeys, whether navigating regulatory uncertainties, overcoming market downturns, or dealing with technical complexities. Their resilience in the face of challenges adds depth to the narratives.

Beyond financial success, many individuals in the crypto space have chosen to leverage their wealth for philanthropic endeavors and innovation. This chapter explores how crypto success stories have contributed to technological advancements, charitable initiatives, and the broader positive impact on society.

The chapter concludes by contemplating the future landscape of crypto investments. It explores emerging trends, potential disruptors, and the evolving narratives that may shape the next generation of success stories in cryptocurrency investments' dynamic and ever-evolving realm.

By examining the diverse journeys of individuals who navigated the complexities of the crypto landscape, readers gain valuable insights, lessons, and motivation for their ventures in the exciting and rapidly evolving world of digital asset investments.

Learning from Mistakes: Lessons from Failures

We are exploring the lessons learned from mistakes, setbacks, and failures within the crypto space. By examining these experiences, we gain valuable insights that can serve as guideposts for seasoned veterans and newcomers navigating the complexities of digital asset investments.

The chapter opens by acknowledging the inherent risks and uncertainties within the cryptocurrency space. Despite the allure of potential rewards, failures, and mistakes are integral to the journey. This section sets the stage for exploring the valuable lessons that can be gleaned from setbacks and missteps.

One common pitfall in the crypto space is overconfidence, leading investors to underestimate the inherent risks. This section delves into case studies where individuals, buoyed by early successes, failed to assess risks, resulting in substantial financial losses adequately. The lesson here is a cautionary tale about the importance of humility and risk management.

Crypto investments often attract attention due to hype and speculative fervor. Refrain from failing fundamental research to make sound investment decisions. This part of the chapter explores instances where investors could not conduct thorough due diligence, relying solely on market sentiment, and paid the price for overlooking the importance of understanding the projects they invested in.

Security breaches and hacks have been unfortunate but prevalent occurrences in crypto. This section highlights instances where lax security practices, such as using insecure wallets or neglecting two-factor authentication, resulted in the loss of funds. The lessons drawn emphasize the importance of prioritizing security in crypto asset management.

The fear of missing out (FOMO) is a powerful force in the crypto market, driving impulsive decisions. This section explores cases where investors succumbed to FOMO, chasing rising prices without a clear strategy, only to face significant losses when market sentiments shifted. The takeaway here is a reminder of the importance of disciplined and strategic investment approaches.

The evolving regulatory landscape presents challenges for crypto investors. Regulatory oversights and non-compliance have led to legal issues and financial losses. This chapter examines cases where individuals neglected regulatory considerations, emphasizing the need to understand the legal framework governing cryptocurrencies.

Centralized exchanges and platforms play a crucial role in the crypto ecosystem. However, blind trust in these platforms has sometimes led to unfortunate outcomes, such as exchange hacks or sudden closures. This section explores cases where users faced financial hardships due to misplaced trust, underscoring the importance of due diligence in choosing service providers.

Failure to diversify and manage portfolios effectively can expose investors to heightened risks. This chapter examines cases where individuals concentrated their investments on a single asset or failed to rebalance portfolios, resulting in disproportionate losses during market downturns. The lesson emphasizes the significance of diversification and prudent portfolio management.

As the chapter concludes, it reflects on the concept of failure not as an endpoint but as a crucial stepping stone to success. The narratives shared serve as testaments to resilience, adaptability, and the capacity for growth that can emerge from learning from mistakes. Embracing failure becomes a transformative aspect of the ongoing journey in the cryptocurrency space.

Understanding these pitfalls and learning from the experiences of others, readers can navigate the complex landscape with greater awareness, resilience, and a foundation for making informed and strategic decisions in their digital asset journeys.

12. The Future of Cryptocurrency

The future of cryptocurrency holds immense promise and potential. This chapter explores the trajectories, trends, and transformative developments shaping the future of digital currencies, blockchain technology, and the broader crypto ecosystem.

The chapter opens with an acknowledgment of cryptocurrencies' revolutionary impact on finance and technology. It sets the stage for exploring the evolving dynamics that will define the future of this rapidly maturing and expanding space.

One of the defining trends in the future of cryptocurrency is the increasing embrace by institutional entities. This section examines how traditional financial institutions, corporations, and governmental bodies integrate cryptocurrencies and blockchain technology, bridging the gap between the crypto niche and mainstream finance.

The rise of Central Bank Digital Currencies represents a pivotal shift in the global financial landscape. This part of the chapter explores the development, adoption, and potential implications of CBDCs, investigating how these government-backed digital currencies may reshape monetary systems and influence the use of traditional fiat currencies.

Decentralized Finance, or DeFi, has emerged as a disruptive force challenging traditional financial intermediaries. This section explores the components of DeFi, including decentralized exchanges, lending platforms, and yield farming. It delves into how this movement is reshaping financial services, fostering financial inclusion, and redefining the concept of ownership and control.

Non-fungible tokens have taken the digital and creative industries by storm. This part of the chapter examines the rise of NFTs, exploring how they are transforming ownership, intellectual property, and digital content monetization. The discussion extends to the potential impact of NFTs on various industries, from art and music to gaming and real estate.

The scalability challenge many blockchain networks face is a crucial aspect of their future viability. This section investigates Layer 2 scaling solutions, such as sidechains and second-layer protocols, and explores the importance of interoperability in creating a cohesive and interconnected blockchain ecosystem.

The environmental impact of cryptocurrency mining has become a topic of global concern. This part of the chapter addresses the challenges associated with energy consumption. It explores potential solutions and initiatives within the crypto community to foster sustainability, including the shift towards Proof-of-Stake consensus mechanisms.

As quantum computing advances, it poses challenges and opportunities for crypto. This section explores the potential implications of quantum computing on cryptographic algorithms and the measures being taken within the industry to prepare for this technological shift.

Regulatory frameworks are evolving to address the growing prominence of cryptocurrencies. This chapter examines how regulatory developments impact the industry, including the balancing act between fostering innovation, protecting consumers, and mitigating risks associated with illicit activities.

As the crypto space advances, community engagement and education become increasingly vital. This section explores how decentralized communities, educational initiatives, and information dissemination contribute to the cryptocurrency ecosystem's continued growth, adoption, and positive evolution.

Emphasizes the dynamic and evolving nature of the crypto space, encouraging readers to stay informed, adaptable, and engaged as they navigate the uncharted territory of this transformative technological landscape.

Emerging Trends in the Crypto Space

The emerging trends are reshaping the digital asset landscape, blockchain technology, and the broader crypto ecosystem. By exploring these trends, readers can gain insights into the forefront of innovation and anticipate the potential shifts that may define the future of the crypto space.

The chapter opens by acknowledging the dynamism of the crypto space and the continuous emergence of new trends. It sets the stage for exploring the latest developments influencing the trajectory of cryptocurrencies and blockchain technology.

Decentralized Autonomous Organizations (DAOs) represent a paradigm shift in organizational structures. This section explores the rise of DAOs, examining how they empower communities to make collective decisions, manage funds, and govern decentralized protocols. A central theme is the potential impact of DAOs on governance and collaboration within the crypto space.

As blockchain ecosystems expand, the need for interoperability becomes increasingly crucial. This part of the chapter investigates the trend of cross-chain compatibility, exploring solutions that enable seamless communication and value transfer between different blockchain networks. The potential benefits and challenges of achieving true interoperability are discussed.

Privacy-focused cryptocurrencies have gained traction as individuals seek greater confidentiality in their transactions. This section explores the rise of privacy coins and the technologies underpinning enhanced confidentiality, such as zero-knowledge proofs and ring signatures. The evolving conversation around privacy and regulatory considerations is also examined.

Environmental sustainability has become a key focus within the crypto space. This chapter delves into emerging trends related to eco-friendly blockchain initiatives, including the rise of sustainable consensus mechanisms, energy-efficient mining practices, and integrating environmental considerations into developing new projects.

The evolution of blockchain technology has paved the way for programmable money and smart contracts. This section explores how these innovations transform traditional financial instruments and contractual agreements, enabling automated and trustless code execution. The potential applications and challenges associated with smart contracts are discussed.

Tokenization is unlocking new possibilities by representing real-world assets on blockchain networks. This chapter explores the trend of tokenizing assets such as real estate, art, and commodities, enabling fractional ownership and enhancing liquidity. The regulatory considerations and potential disruptions to traditional financial systems are examined.

Building on the success of the initial DeFi wave, DeFi 2.0 represents a new chapter in decentralized finance. This section explores emerging trends within DeFi, including integrating traditional financial instruments, algorithmic stablecoins, and enhanced risk management strategies. The potential for continued innovation and the challenges faced by the DeFi sector are discussed.

Non-fungible tokens (NFTs) have expanded beyond the realm of digital art. This part of the chapter explores the diversification of NFT use cases, including gaming, music, virtual real estate applications, and the metaverse. The potential impact on various industries and the challenges associated with broader NFT adoption are examined.

The intersection of blockchain and artificial intelligence is opening up new possibilities. This section explores the emerging trend of integrating AI with blockchain technology, examining use cases such as predictive analytics, fraud detection, and decentralized AI marketplaces. The potential synergies and ethical considerations are discussed.

Regulatory and compliance solutions are becoming increasingly important as the crypto space matures. This part of the chapter explores emerging trends in regulatory technology (RegTech) within the crypto industry, including tools for identity verification, transaction monitoring, and regulatory reporting. The evolving relationship between regulators and the crypto sector is also examined.

It emphasizes the need for continuous awareness, adaptability, and a forward-thinking mindset as participants navigate the ever-evolving landscape of digital assets, blockchain technology, and the broader cryptocurrency ecosystem.

Predictions for the Future of Cryptocurrency

Peering into the future of cryptocurrency is both challenging and exhilarating, given the dynamic nature of the space. This chapter explores a series of predictions that encapsulate the potential trajectories, innovations, and transformative developments that could shape the future of cryptocurrencies, blockchain technology, and the broader crypto ecosystem.

The chapter opens with recognizing the speculative nature of predicting the future. It sets the stage for exploring the potential trends and developments that may unfold in the ever-evolving world of cryptocurrencies.

One prediction centers around the increasing mainstream adoption of cryptocurrencies. This section explores the potential scenarios where digital assets become more widely accepted as a means of payment, traditional financial institutions fully embrace crypto services, and individuals seamlessly integrate cryptocurrencies into their daily economic activities.

The emergence of Central Bank Digital Currencies (CBDCs) is poised to become a prominent feature of the financial landscape. This part of the chapter explores predictions about the widespread issuance and adoption of CBDCs, examining the potential implications for monetary policy, financial inclusion, and the relationship between traditional and digital currencies.

Decentralized Finance (DeFi) has the potential to mature into a sophisticated financial ecosystem. This section delves into predictions regarding the evolution of DeFi protocols, integrating traditional financial instruments, and establishing regulatory frameworks that foster innovation while addressing potential risks.

Privacy and security are likely to be at the forefront of technological developments. This part of the chapter explores predictions about advancements in privacy-focused cryptocurrencies, the integration of enhanced security measures, and the development of protocols that address data protection and confidentiality concerns.

Tokenization is expected to extend its reach beyond traditional asset classes. This section explores predictions about tokenizing a broader range of real-world assets, including intellectual property, commodities, and conventional financial instruments. The potential impact on liquidity, ownership structures, and market accessibility is considered.

The convergence of artificial intelligence (AI) and blockchain technology is anticipated to yield transformative outcomes. This part of the chapter explores predictions regarding the integration of AI into blockchain networks, examining use cases such as decentralized AI marketplaces, predictive analytics, and fraud detection.

The Non-Fungible Token (NFT) space will witness continued evolution and diversification. This section explores predictions about expanding NFT use cases beyond art, encompassing industries such as gaming, music, virtual real estate, and the broader metaverse.

As quantum computing advances, the need for quantum-resistant cryptography becomes more pressing. This part of the chapter explores predictions related to the development and integration of quantum-resistant cryptographic algorithms, safeguarding the security of blockchain networks in the face of evolving computational capabilities.

Regulatory frameworks will likely evolve to provide more precise guidelines for the crypto industry. This section explores predictions about increased regulatory clarity, adopting standardized compliance solutions, and collaborative efforts between regulators and industry participants to foster innovation while mitigating risks.

Environmental sustainability is anticipated to be a priority for the blockchain industry. This part of the chapter explores predictions related to the widespread adoption of sustainable practices, including the shift towards eco-friendly consensus mechanisms, energy-efficient mining practices, and initiatives to reduce the carbon footprint of blockchain networks.

The evolution of the internet into Web 3.0, characterized by decentralized, user-centric applications, is predicted to unfold. This section explores how blockchain technology may be central in shaping Web 3.0, fostering greater user control, data privacy, and a more decentralized Internet infrastructure.

The speculative nature of foresight in the dynamic crypto landscape encourages stakeholders to stay informed, adaptive, and forward-thinking as they navigate the uncharted territories of digital assets, blockchain technology, and the broader cryptocurrency ecosystem.

Adapting to Changes in the Crypto Market

Adaptability is a crucial ingredient for success in the ever-evolving cryptocurrency market landscape. Explores the strategies and mindset required to navigate the dynamic changes, challenges, and opportunities that characterize the crypto space. By understanding the principles of adaptability, investors and enthusiasts can position themselves to thrive in a market known for its volatility and innovation.

The chapter begins by acknowledging the crypto market's inherent volatility and rapid evolution. It sets the stage for exploring the importance of adaptability and the strategies that individuals and organizations can employ to thrive in an environment subject to continuous change.

Adaptability starts with a mindset. This section delves into the concept of a growth mindset, emphasizing embracing challenges as opportunities for learning and growth. It explores how cultivating a mindset that welcomes change can position individuals to adapt more effectively to shifts in the crypto market.

Staying informed is a cornerstone of adaptability in the crypto market. This chapter explores the importance of continuous learning, tracking market trends, and staying abreast of technological developments. It highlights the role of information gathering as a strategic tool for making informed decisions in the face of market changes.

Diversification is a fundamental strategy for adapting to market changes. This section explores diversifying crypto portfolios across different assets, industries, and risk profiles. It discusses how a diversified approach can help mitigate risk and position investors to weather market fluctuations.

The crypto market operates 24/7, and conditions can change rapidly. This chapter emphasizes the importance of active monitoring and regular reassessment of investment portfolios. It explores how staying vigilant to market trends and adjusting strategies can be crucial for adapting to changing market dynamics.

Trading strategies that may have been successful in one market condition may be less effective in another. This section explores the need for flexibility in trading strategies, including the ability to adapt to different market phases, such as bull markets, bear markets, and periods of consolidation.

Risk is inherent in the crypto market, and effective risk mitigation requires careful planning. This part of the chapter delves into the importance of contingency planning, including setting stop-loss orders, having exit strategies, and being prepared for unexpected events. It explores how risk mitigation measures contribute to adaptability in market uncertainties.

The crypto community is valuable for information, support, and collaboration. This section explores the role of community engagement and networking in adapting to market changes. It highlights the benefits of connecting with fellow enthusiasts, industry professionals, and thought leaders to share insights and collectively navigate market shifts.

Regulatory changes can significantly impact the crypto market. This part of the chapter explores the importance of regulatory awareness and compliance. It discusses how staying informed about evolving regulatory frameworks and ensuring compliance with legal requirements contribute to adaptability and long-term sustainability.

Technological advancements are a driving force in the crypto space. This section explores the importance of technology adoption and innovation for staying competitive. It emphasizes how embracing new technologies, such as blockchain upgrades or improvements in security measures, can enhance adaptability and keep participants at the forefront of the market.

The crypto market's volatility can test the emotional resilience of participants. This chapter explores the significance of psychological resilience and emotional intelligence in adapting to market changes. It discusses strategies for managing emotions, overcoming setbacks, and maintaining a balanced approach to decision-making in the face of market fluctuations.

It reinforces the importance of a growth mindset, continuous learning, risk management, community engagement, and technological innovation. By internalizing these principles, individuals, and organizations can position themselves to adapt to changes and thrive in the dynamic and ever-evolving crypto ecosystem.

Conclusion

As we draw the final pages of "CRYPTO RICH: Transforming Investments into Crypto Millions," it becomes evident that the journey into the world of cryptocurrencies is both exhilarating and transformative. Throughout this exploration, we've uncovered the stories of individuals who ventured into crypto, transformed their investments, and emerged as Crypto Millionaires. As we conclude this chapter, let's reflect on the key takeaways and the overarching message that resonates from these tales of crypto wealth creation.

"Crypto Rich" is not just a title but a testament to the transformative power of cryptocurrencies. The individuals featured in these pages embraced the evolution of wealth creation, leveraging blockchain technology's decentralized and innovative nature to rewrite the rules of financial success.

A recurring theme throughout this journey is the significance of mindset. The Crypto Millionaires showcased in this book exhibited a growth mindset, embracing challenges, learning from mistakes, and adapting to the ever-changing crypto market dynamics. They approached investments with a forward-thinking attitude, seeing opportunities where others might see risks.

Crypto wealth doesn't have a one-size-fits-all formula. The stories shared in "CRYPTO RICH" underscore the diversity of strategies employed by individuals to accumulate their fortunes. From early Bitcoin adopters to DeFi enthusiasts, from strategic traders to those navigating the ICO boom, the crypto landscape offers a multitude of paths to financial success.

Acknowledging the importance of learning from mistakes, we explored pitfalls and challenges faced by Crypto Millionaires. The chapter on failures underscored that setbacks are not the end but stepping stones to future success. It emphasized the resilience and adaptability required to navigate the uncertainties of the crypto journey.

As we conclude this book, it's crucial to recognize that the crypto landscape is still unfolding. Predictions for the future, emerging trends, and the need for adaptability all point to an environment that will continue to surprise, challenge, and reward those who dare to venture into the realm of digital assets.

While "CRYPTO RICH" has delved into financial success stories, it's important to note that becoming crypto-rich extends beyond monetary wealth. The crypto community is a vibrant and collaborative space where innovation, technological advancements, and the potential for positive societal impact are equally significant rewards.

In closing, "CRYPTO RICH" is not just a narrative of financial success but a guide to adopting the Crypto Mindset, embracing the evolution of wealth, and navigating the dynamic crypto landscape. Whether you're a seasoned investor, a newcomer to the crypto space, or someone simply curious about the future of finance, may the stories and lessons within these pages inspire and guide you on your journey to crypto riches. As the crypto adventure continues, remember: the next chapter is waiting to be written, and the possibilities are as limitless as the blockchain.

Appendix

Congratulations on embarking on the transformative journey outlined in "CRYPTO RICH: Transforming Investments into Crypto Millions." This appendix serves as a comprehensive resource guide, providing readers with valuable tools, platforms, and references to further enhance their understanding of the crypto landscape and support their endeavors in the digital asset space.

1. Educational Platforms:**

 Crypto Courses and Certifications:**
 [Coursera] (https://www.coursera.org/)
 [Udemy] (https://www.udemy.com/)
 [Blockchain at Berkeley] (https://blockchain.berkeley.edu/)

Online Blogs and Articles:
 [CoinDesk] (https://www.coindesk.com/)
 [Cointelegraph] (https://cointelegraph.com/)
 [The Block] (https://www.theblockcrypto.com/)

YouTube Channels:
 [Andreas M. Antonopoulos]
(https://www.youtube.com/user/aantonop)
 [DataDash](https://www.youtube.com/c/DataDash)
 [CryptoCandor](https://www.youtube.com/c/CryptoCandor)

2. Trading and Investment Platforms:

 Cryptocurrency Exchanges:**
 [Binance] (https://www.binance.com/)
 [Coinbase] (https://www.coinbase.com/)
 [Kraken] (https://r.kraken.com/c/2042870/687155/10583)

Portfolio Management Tools:
  [Blockfolio] (https://www.blockfolio.com/)
  [Delta] (https://getdelta.io/)

Trading Analysis Platforms:
  [TradingView] (https://www.tradingview.com/)
  [Coinigy] (https://www.coinigy.com/)

Security and Wallets:

Hardware Wallets:
  [Ledger](https://www.ledger.com/)
  [Trezor] (https://trezor.io/)

Software Wallets:
  [MyEtherWallet] (https://www.myetherwallet.com/)
  Exodus] (https://www.exodus.com/)

Security Best Practices:
  [Crypto Security Guide]v(https://cryptosec.info/)

4. Regulatory and Compliance Resources:

Regulatory News and Updates:
  [Coin Center] (https://coincenter.org/)
  [Blockchain Association] (https://www.blockchainassociation.io/)

Compliance Solutions:
  [CipherTrace] (https://ciphertrace.com/)
  [Chainalysis] (https://www.chainalysis.com/)

5. Community and Networking:

Forums and Communities:
  [BitcoinTalk](https://bitcointalk.org/)

[CryptoCompare] (https://www.cryptocompare.com/)

Conferences and Events:
 [Consensus] (https://www.coindesk.com/events/consensus-2023)
 [Blockchain Summit] (https://www.blockchainsummit.io/)

6. Further Reading:

Books on Cryptocurrency:
 Mastering Bitcoin by Andreas M. Antonopoulos
 The Bitcoin Standard by Saifedean Ammous
 Blockchain Basics by Daniel Drescher

Research Papers:
 [Bitcoin Whitepaper](https://bitcoin.org/bitcoin.pdf)
 [Ethereum Whitepaper] (https://ethereum.org/en/whitepaper/)

7. Emerging Technologies:

Decentralized Finance (DeFi) Platforms:
 [Aave] (https://aave.com/)
 [Uniswap] (https://uniswap.org/)

Non-Fungible Token (NFT) Platforms:
 [OpenSea] (https://opensea.io/)
 - [Rarible](https://rarible.com/)

8. Podcasts and Media:

Crypto Podcasts:
 [The Pomp Podcast] (https://pomp.substack.com/)
 [Unchained] (https://www.coindesk.com/podcasts/unchained)

Crypto News Outlets:
 [Decrypt](https://decrypt.co/)

[CoinJournal](https://coinjournal.net/)

These resources are curated to provide a comprehensive foundation for anyone seeking to navigate the crypto landscape. Keep in mind that the crypto world is dynamic, and staying informed and engaged will be key to your continued success. Happy exploring, and may your crypto journey be rich with knowledge and prosperity!